A PILGRIM PATH:

John Bunyan's journey

A NEW BIOGRAPHY BY FAITH COOK

BOOKS

EP BOOKS

EP Books (Evangelical Press), Registered Office: 140 Coniscliffe Road, Darlington, Co Durham DL3 7RT
admin@epbooks.org
www.epbooks.org

EP Books are distributed in the USA by:
JPL Books, 3883 Linden Ave. S.E., Wyoming, MI 49548
order@jplbooks.com
www.jplbooks.com

British Library Cataloguing in Publication Data available
ISBN 978-1-78397-213-5

CONTENTS

CHAPTER 1

A TROUBLED YOUTH

Only four years had passed since Thomas Bunyan had first married Anne, a girl from his home village of Elstow in Bedfordshire, and now she had died. Perhaps he felt unable to cope alone because just two months later he remarried. Thomas already knew Margaret Bentley for she too was from Elstow, then a straggling village of only sixty-one cottages lying just a mile and a half from Bedford. Both were born in 1603, and with their homes all clustering around the village green, must have played together as children, sharing any education available to village children at the time. Now twenty-four, they married and set up home together in old Harrowden, an area on the outer fringes of Elstow.

Their thatched wattle-and-daub cottage had only one living room with a rickety staircase leading up to several bedrooms. Immediately adjacent to his cottage Thomas had built a forge where he could hammer out the metals needed for his living—mending pots and pans—for he was a brazier by trade, more popularly known as a tinker.

And it was in this cottage that Thomas and Margaret's first child was born in November 1628. Today the site of the child's birth is marked by a memorial stone in the far corner of a field of wheat near a reedy stream known as Elstow Brook. Driving slowly along the A421 near Bedford, an observant passenger may pick out the stone in the distance and even ask the driver to stop and take a photograph. But why the interest in the birth of the son of a poor tinker and his wife in a rural Bedfordshire village almost four hundred years ago? Little could

Thomas and Margaret know that this son of theirs—John Bunyan—would find a place in the annals of secular and religious history long after many princes, rulers, politicians and church leaders had been long forgotten. A baptismal record states briefly: *John, the sonne of Thomas Bonnionn Jun., the 30th of Novemb.*

THE CALM BEFORE THE STORM

The placid Bedfordshire countryside may have looked calm enough that November in 1628, when John was born, but far off in London a serious situation was developing. England was in turmoil, religiously, socially and economically with the king, Charles I, on a collision course with his Parliament. English men and women had long memories. Some had grandparents who could remember the reign of Mary Tudor, known as Bloody Queen Mary, an ardent Roman Catholic who sent some of the noblest citizens of the land to a fiery and fearful death at the stake for their Protestant faith. Many could remember a more recent event that had occurred only twenty-three years ago. In November 1605 Guy Fawkes and his cronies had attempted to blow up the king and his House of Commons, in order to provoke anarchy in the hope of subsequently setting another Catholic monarch on the throne. Small wonder then that the people were uneasy and not a little anxious because Charles I, aided and abetted by William Laud, soon to be Archbishop, was displaying strong Roman Catholic sympathies.

With an intense belief in the divine right of kings Charles simply dismissed his parliaments when they refused to give him money for wars and projects which they felt to be against the country's best interests. Then at last in 1628, the very year of John's birth, things came to a head with Parliament issuing Charles with an ultimatum—a Petition of Rights. Four severe abuses, either condoned or practiced by Charles, lay at the heart of Parliament's demands. If these were dealt with, then Parliament would agree to grant the funds which Charles requested for his wars. Unwillingly the king acceded to the Petition, but before dealing with the issues he had dismissed his Parliament yet again and would reign alone for the next eleven years—a situation that led directly to the outbreak of the fearful Civil War in 1642, a war that ripped the country apart, turning neighbour against neighbour and even father against son.

Meanwhile a second child, a daughter, also named Margaret like her mother, was born into the Bunyan home and three years later another son, William, completed the family. But the England into which the Bunyan children had been born was marked by inflexible social distinctions with little chance of a poor man ever improving his lot in life. To the Bunyan family the sight of the magnificent newly-built Elstow Place, home of Sir Thomas Hillersdon, vividly demonstrated this fact as it dwarfed the nearby villagers' cottages. Each Sunday, as the family made its way to church across Elstow Green and on into the dim recesses of the high-vaulted Abbey Church, they would pass the grand Hillersdon residence. Week by week the vast gulf between the privileged few and the peasant majority was being forcibly impressed upon them.

YOUNGER DAYS AND LEARNING

Although Thomas Bunyan was unable to write, later signing his own will with a thumbprint, he was far-sighted and self-denying enough to decide that John should have the advantage of a basic education. Perhaps they had already detected in the boy the stirrings of a remarkable intellect, for John records:

> *It pleased God to put it into their hearts to put me to school to learn both to read and write; the which I also attained, according to the rate of other poor men's children.*

John would probably have learnt his alphabet with the help of a horn book, as was common in both Tudor and Stuart times. Mounted on a wooden frame, this primer, made of horn, contained the alphabet written in upper and lower case, a benediction and the Lord's Prayer.

But young John Bunyan was not an easy child to handle. A strong character, physically tall and hardy, with distinctive reddish hair, he soon became a ringleader amongst the boys of Elstow. Undoubtedly he enjoyed the rough games

of a primitive type of football played on the village green. The record he leaves
of his childhood days suggests that Thomas and Margaret Bunyan did little to
restrain their son's erratic and wild behaviour. He tells us in a frank admission
of his unruly conduct:

> *I had but few equals especially considering my years, which
> were tender, being few, both for cursing, swearing, lying and
> blaspheming the holy name of God.*

He gives no hint that such language grieved his parents; indeed, he may well
have first learnt it from them. Like many who blaspheme without scruple or
conscience, such language became habitual to the boy as he tells:

> *Yea, so settled and rooted was I in these things that they became
> as a second nature to me.*

Little evidence remains to suggest that Thomas and Margaret Bunyan were
anything other than formal in their religious views, but Sunday by Sunday, in
keeping with the legal requirements of the day, they were to be found in their
appointed seats in the church. We cannot know what sort of sermons the children heard from the vicar, John Kellie, but certainly John was early made aware
of the spiritual realm: of heaven, of hell and the coming judgement of God
against sin. A child with a vivid imagination, he later recognized the restraining
hand of God in the alarming dreams that began to trouble him at this time. He
has left us a graphic description:

> *I ... did so offend the Lord that even in my childhood he did
> scare and affright me with fearful dreams, and did terrify me
> with dreadful visions.*

After each thoughtless day when blasphemies, lies and curses had poured out of
his mouth, John faced a nightly retribution:

> *I have in my bed been greatly afflicted, while asleep, with the
> apprehensions of devils and wicked spirits, who still, as I then*

*thought, laboured to draw me away with them, of which I
could never be rid.*

John's capacity for heights of elation and depths of distress coupled with a powerful imagination is evident even in these early years of his life. Suddenly, as he was cheerfully playing with his friends, his mind would cloud over with dark and stormy thoughts:

*These things, I say, when I was but a child but nine or ten years
old, did so distress my soul that when in the midst of my many
sports and childish vanities, amidst my vain companions, I was
often much cast down and afflicted in my mind therewith, yet
could I not let go my sins.*

Troubled about his lawless behaviour, John describes a frightening alternative that occurred to him:

*I was also then so overcome with despair of life and heaven that
I should often wish either that there had been no hell, or that
I had been a devil — supposing they were only tormentors —
that if it must needs be that I went thither, I might be rather a
tormentor, than be tormented myself.*

Meanwhile, John Bunyan's education came to an abrupt end when he was about nine years old. He had mastered the rudiments of reading and writing, but now his father needed him in the forge to assist with the work, so aiding the family finances. Also it was time for him to begin his seven-year apprenticeship, which was necessary if he wished to carry on the business or to set up as a brazier on his own account.

Referring to his education, John confesses regretfully, 'I did soon lose that little I learned, and that even almost utterly.' Despite such a claim, it is evident from other comments he makes that during his youth he much enjoyed reading the novels, or 'chapbooks', of the day. *George on Horseback* and *Bevis of Southampton* were among John's favourite stories. Such tales of heroism appeal to boys of any generation, and they left indelible marks on John's imagination.

But by the time John had entered his teenage years he had managed to harden his mind against the frightening reminders of God's displeasure against his sin, and soon his terrifying dreams died out. He was able, or so it seemed, to act and speak as badly as he wished without any painful pangs of conscience, delighting, 'in all transgression against the law of God'. Later he would confess sadly, 'I was one of these great sin-breeders; I infected all the youth of the town where I was born with all manner of youthful vanities.'

There were also highlights of Bunyan's childhood . One was the Elstow Fair. Dating from the early twelfth century, fairs had been held annually on Elstow Green during the first week of May. These occasions, although including dances around a maypole, were not primarily designed for amusement, as many fairs are today. They were more like a busy outdoor market, with local traders shouting the virtues of their wares from behind their stalls.

The Moot Hall, built about one hundred years before John's birth and still a notable landmark for visitors to Elstow today, was originally designed to provide storage for the equipment and stalls used for the fair. Then known as the Green House, it was also a makeshift court to resolve disputes arising from the fair: faulty merchandise, complaints about suspect weights and measures, and wrangles between rival salesmen. Little wonder that a village boy like John would have been intrigued to mingle with the crowds and watch all that was going on.

EARLY SPIRITUAL EXPERIENCES

Although John Bunyan managed to neglect and forget God, God had not forgotten him. On two or three occasions he was remarkably preserved from imminent danger. As a non-swimmer he records an episode when the small boat he was in capsized in the River Ouse in Bedford. How he struggled ashore, or whether someone stretched out a kindly hand to help him, we do not know, but the incident remained stamped on his mind for many years. Later he would recognize God's merciful protection watching over him.

On another occasion John began to show off to a friend after catching sight of an adder slithering across the road. With reckless daring John stunned the reptile with a blow from the stick in his hand. Then the foolish youth forced open the snake's mouth with his stick, put his fingers down its throat and pulled out the adder's sting. 'Had not God been merciful unto me,' Bunyan comments, 'I might by my desperateness have brought myself to mine end.'

An intelligent boy, John must certainly have been aware of the alarming build-up in tensions on the national scene as the country teetered towards civil war with a fatal confrontation between Charles I and his Parliament. He may well have heard of the angry demonstrations in 1637 in the Palace Yard in London as men of influence and distinction were pilloried and mutilated for their refusal to pay the extortionate taxes being levied by the king—taxes that also angered Bedfordshire men.

As a lover of adventure stories, the twelve-year-old cannot fail to have been thrilled when two thousand local men marched to London on 16 March 1641. Four abreast they passed through Elstow, which lay on the high road to the capital. Displayed on their hats were the words of the petition they were carrying to the reconvened House of Commons, protesting against exploitation, evil and corrupt councillors, together with the unacceptable religious ceremonials. Doubtless John would have been eager to find out the reason for such protests.

But by the following year protests had turned to the regular tramp of feet as soldiers began to muster for the forthcoming conflict. Perhaps young Bunyan, now steadily employed in his father's forge, looked with longing as the conscripts marched through Elstow, and felt his pulse quicken at the thought that one day he too might possibly become a soldier.

Another year would pass, however, before, in the late spring of 1644, a situation arose in Elstow and the surrounding district which put all such thoughts far from John's mind. A terrifying epidemic broke out in the community, sweeping young and old indiscriminately to their graves. Who would be next to develop the alarming symptoms and die? It was a question on everyone's lips. We can only imagine the distress in the small cottage by the stream in Harrowden when John's mother, Margaret, fell ill and died at the age of forty-one. John was fifteen at the time, his sister, Margaret, only thirteen and William was eleven—all at an age when their need of a mother's love and care was at its most acute.

As the small funeral procession wound its way across the fields to Elstow churchyard on 20 June 1644, John could not have guessed that little more than a month later he would once again tread that same painful track as his young sister Margaret, his childhood companion, was also carried to her grave. The boy's desolation of spirit is not hard to imagine as both his mother and sister were taken in so short a space of time. All of the softening influences in the youth's life had vanished at a stroke.

And, as if that were not hard enough, within a month another woman was in his mother's bed. Unable to sustain his home and his business without Margaret, Thomas Bunyan had hastily remarried just weeks after his wife's death. He cannot have given any due consideration for the feelings of his two boys, John and William. Little wonder then that John Bunyan threw himself into further youthful abandon. Now he could say:

> *In these days the thoughts of religion were very grievous to me;*
> *I could neither endure it myself, nor that any other should…*
> *Then I said unto God 'Depart from me for I desire not the*
> *knowledge of thy ways'*

But out of all these unpromising circumstances God was at work, forming this young man into one whom he would use some day to bring glory to his name.

CHAPTER 2

A SOLDIER'S LOT

As the people of Elstow and the surrounding area struggled against the deadly ravages of disease, and John Bunyan grieved the death of his mother and sister, a tragedy of still greater proportions was unfolding in the north of England. Just twelve days after his mother's funeral, more than four thousand young men were lying dead on a battlefield outside Long Marston, an area known as Marston Moor, seven miles west of the city of York.

War between Parliament and the King had broken out. But what had happened to bring about this grievous situation, where neighbours were killing neighbours, and fathers their sons? Writers still argue about the long-term causes of the Civil War that started in the summer of 1642. But few would disagree with the historian Paul Johnson that the England of 1640 'seemed in ruins. It was spiritually, morally and physically bankrupt. It had lost its soul… All the ancient and familiar landmarks had gone.'

The immediate cause of war was the final breakdown between Charles I and his Parliament, which he had recalled in 1640 to supply funds to help him fight the Scots. Before supplying any money, Parliament had grievances of its own which it wished to see redressed. The king, unwilling to satisfy such demands or to undertake any reformation of the many ills that plagued the country, had answered Parliament's complaints by raising his standard at Nottingham on 22 August 1642, declaring war on his own people.

John Bunyan was fourteen at the time and, as a youth with natural leadership ability and deep feelings, he would have followed all these events as much as he was able. Bedfordshire as a county was solidly behind the Parliamentarian cause. Two years of inconclusive fighting had followed, with heavy losses on both sides, but now, after that decisive victory of Marston Moor in 1644, the tide was definitely turning in Parliament's favour. The Scots had been coaxed to enter the war on the Parliamentary side in 1643, on condition that Parliament agreed to work together with the Scottish church towards uniformity of religion, by establishing a Presbyterian system of church order in the English churches.

Despite the undoubted help of the Scottish army under Sir Alexander Leslie, reinforcements were still urgently needed to make good Parliament's losses. As Sir Thomas Fairfax, the commander-in-chief, was demanding the recruitment of another 14,000 men, agents were sent throughout the country to conscript any young men aged sixteen or over who appeared able-bodied. Some were press-ganged; others may have volunteered. In the autumn of 1644 Sir Samuel Luke, MP for Bedford and in charge of the garrison at Newport Pagnell, twelve miles from Bedford, arrived in Elstow searching for recruits.

A tall, tough-looking youth with bright eyes, a sharp intelligent face and distinctive auburn hair attracted his attention. Not yet sixteen, John Bunyan was too young to be conscripted, but he may well have looked older and could therefore have been forced into armed service. The likelihood, however, is that one as adept at lying as Bunyan would have had no difficulty in saying that he was sixteen. Besides, his home life had become far from happy since his mother's death and his father's remarriage. Perhaps life in the army would provide an escape from a difficult situation. So in October 1644 John found himself marching the twelve miles to the garrison town of Newport Pagnell with a contingent of other conscripts. Here he was to be stationed, at least for the present.

A new and highly significant phase of his life had begun. But if John thought that the life of a soldier would be an escape route from the bleak circumstances he faced at home, he was sadly mistaken. Uncongenial as his home might have been, the experiences he would meet in army life must have made him wish he had remained unnoticed when Sir Samuel Luke's agents came to Elstow.

Newport Pagnell is a small market town that can trace its origins to the Iron Age; its strategic position, cradled between two rivers, the River Ouse and its tributary the River Lovat, gave it a natural defence against any invaders. Equally important was the fact that the Ouse could be forded at that point. By the time the Domesday Book was compiled in 1086, Newport Pagnell was one of the more important towns in the country. Early in the Civil War, Charles I's generals had seen the importance of gaining a foothold there and using it as a garrison town from which they could launch an attack on the capital. Consequently, Sir Lewis Dyve had been commissioned to occupy Newport Pagnell for the king.

But the Earl of Essex, lord-general of the Parliamentary forces, also had his eye on the place, seeing it as a significant fortification against incursions from the north, where the Royalists were strong, and also as a useful supply route to London. In October 1643 Essex and his troops advanced towards the town, but to their amazement discovered that Sir Lewis Dyve had inexplicably evacuated, together with all his men. Later it was discovered that he had misunderstood a message from the king and thought he was being ordered to leave Newport Pagnell.

John Bunyan was stationed in Colonel Richard Cokayne's company, which consisted of 128 'centinells', or foot soldiers, together with their officers, under the overall authority of Sir Samuel Luke, Governor of the town. A foot soldier's main weapon was a sword and, when supplies permitted, a musket as well. Each week Cokayne was supposed to fill in a muster roll recording the names of those men serving under him, so enabling him to claim the pay due to them for that week. John Bunyan's name first appears on the Newport Pagnell muster rolls on his birthday, 30 November 1644, but, as earlier records appear to be missing, he may well have been present in the town for several months already. Soon after their arrival new recruits were issued with a copy of *The Souldiers Pocket Bible*.

Apart from the novels he had read, this would probably be the first real 'book' John had possessed.

The Souldiers Pocket Bible consisted of some twelve pages and was about the size of a modern passport. First issued in 1643, this slim booklet contained a selection of 150 verses, all but four from the Old Testament and chosen mainly to encourage and instruct a soldier. A fighting man could easily slip it down his long boots or hide it in some pocket.

Collected under sixteen short headings, John would read such instructions as: 'A Souldier must not do wickedly...'; 'A souldier must be valiant for God's Cause...'; 'A Souldier must pray before he go to fight'—each with an appropriate verse of Scripture attached. Whether John paid much attention to these things is doubtful. Commenting on his army days, Bunyan tells us that neither judgments nor mercy 'did awaken my soul to righteousness; wherefore I sinned still, and grew more and more rebellious against God, and careless of mine own salvation'.

The entire garrison was made up of about 800 foot soldiers although Sir Samuel had hoped to recruit 1,200. Ordinary 'centinells' were supposed to receive eight pence a day as pay from their respective home counties. But if those counties were reluctant to forward the necessary funds, or reneged on their responsibilities, the soldiers obviously suffered. Pay was hopelessly in arrears at the time that John first enrolled, giving rise to acute problems.

Unable to cover basic costs, the army quickly incurred the antagonism of the locals who were expected to accommodate the soldiers in their homes. Some nasty situations developed. A document has survived dated 14 April 1645, after Bunyan had been in the army for about six months, in which forty-one soldiers were petitioning Sir Samuel Luke urgently for money. They claimed that if they deferred paying for their accommodation any longer, 'the people may rise and cut our throats', and, as if that were not bad enough, they added that they had 'no clothes, no ammunition or supplies for their horses.'

Not surprisingly, scavenging and looting became commonplace. When bands of soldiers were sent out on forays against local Royalist units, prisoners were captured and brought back to the town. In many instances their clothes and personal possessions were stolen and sold. To raise money for food some men even pawned articles of their own clothing which they could scarcely spare.

Sometimes officers lent money to the men to pay for essential supplies, but accounts are extant in letters written by the governor, Sir Samuel Luke, describing the desperate situation in Newport Pagnell. 'The men have neither boots for their legs nor money to buy shoes for their horses.' He went on to describe a case of two soldiers who had to share a single pair of breeches; when one man wore the trousers the other was obliged to remain in bed all day. So cold was it that many soldiers, having no coats, refused to leave their beds at all; while at other times a shortage of townsfolk prepared to give the men accommodation could lead to three soldiers having to share one bed.

Adequate weapons were equally hard to obtain, even though Sir Samuel continually sent urgent letters to London requesting further supplies of muskets, pikes, pistols, horses and boots for the men. In such circumstances many soldiers tried to abscond and return home. Only the threat of immediate death by hanging on one of the local gibbets prevented more men from trying such an expedient. It is not hard to imagine that John Bunyan, a youth of barely sixteen, would have been dismayed at such circumstances, but we have no record of any attempt on his part to return to Elstow. Hardy and used to tough conditions, he was not the sort to succumb to such deprivations.

While these conditions provided an ideal opportunity for many to attempt a defection from the Parliamentary army, we are not surprised to learn that in December 1644 some in the town who were still loyal to Charles I sent him a secret message informing him of the dire situation there. Scarcely more than 200 soldiers, so they reported, were still in the garrison at that time; morale was at rock bottom and even the bulwarks and outer defences were crumbling. The king could hardly wish for a better moment to mount an attack and regain the town for the Royalist cause.

In the light of such intelligence, Charles and his army advanced on Newport Pagnell. John Bunyan had not been in the garrison for more than a couple of months, with little opportunity for military training, before it appeared that he was about to have his first taste of armed combat. Sir Samuel scarcely knew what to do in the circumstances. News had arrived that '... his majesty's army both horse and foot are marching this way and were quartering last night within less than 20 miles.' If he left the garrison to seek additional troops, he feared that 'the remaining soldiers, for want of pay, would most of them disband… Besides my absence might encourage the enemy to come on.' All he could do was to write urgently to a nearby garrison for reinforcements.

In the event only bitter weather prevented the king from taking further advantage of the plight of Newport Pagnell and of Sir Samuel Luke's men. At least the imminent threat produced one useful result: when the board appointed by Parliament to oversee the war strategy heard how nearly their Newport Pagnell garrison could have been lost, it immediately sent £500 to relieve the situation.

Although John Bunyan had not yet tasted the bitterness of military conflict, or experienced the horror of Englishmen being called upon to kill Englishmen, he had already had to cope with a degree of deprivation and hardship which he would never forget. A soldier's lot was certainly not a happy one.

CHAPTER 3

A BABBLE OF VOICES

L ife in the armed forces brought young John Bunyan into contact with a wide range of new ideas and religious opinions. Amid the babble of voices there were many who propounded ideas that were far from biblical. For a village boy like John, the torrent of different opinions that he met in day-to-day army life must have been an immense culture shock at first. Here he encountered men of contradictory ideologies far removed from those he had heard in childhood as he sat under the sermons of John Kellie.

Doubtless John, who later describes himself as 'a brisk talker', also found himself at the heart of many heated debates, political as well as religious, as he lounged around the garrison. The news from home was that his stepmother had just given birth to a son, controversially enough named Charles, suggesting that his father supported the Royalist cause. To name the new baby 'Charles' was tactless at best on Thomas Bunyan's part, since his oldest son was fighting with the Parliamentary army, and it can only have been a further grievance for John. Sceptical and profane in his own use of language, the young man is not likely to have been one of Sir Samuel Luke's favourite soldiers!

While Archbishop Laud and his High Church rituals had dominated church life in the 1630s, individual opinions had been suppressed. But with Parliament back in control and past scores to settle, the old bishop was accused of betraying the Protestant faith and therefore of treason. Now over seventy he was first incarcerated in the Tower of London, and then beheaded in January 1645. John Bunyan was just seventeen at the time. A religious free-for-all followed with every one appearing to have a different viewpoint, some wild and confused, while others promoting true godliness. Restrictions on publishers were lifted and the market flooded with books and pamphlets, most of them on controversial subjects. Newspapers were no longer illegal, with more than 700 different ones appearing in 1645 alone. Little wonder that soldiers like young Bunyan were confused.

With the death of Laud the pace of change accelerated, particularly after the formation of Oliver Cromwell's New Model Army with its generals now appointed for ability and religious convictions rather than noble birth and prestige. Sir Thomas Fairfax, a just and brilliant general, was chosen as Lord-General of the New Model Army and confirmed by Parliament in April 1645. Under Fairfax the New Model Army was quickly moulded into an efficient, disciplined fighting force.

Of more direct relevance to Bunyan was the decision of Parliament to change the structure of pay for men serving in the army. Alarmed at the number absconding and the near mutinies over arrears of pay, Parliament decided that in future the soldiers' pay was to come from national rather than local taxes, and by the autumn of 1645 the situation at Newport Pagnell had improved considerably.

But did John Bunyan actually see any action during his years in the Parliamentary army, a question often posed? Those, like Bunyan, who protected the various garrisons during the Civil War were not part of the fighting units engaged in the great set-piece battles such as Marston Moor. But theirs too was a dangerous assignment as they regularly sallied forth on local missions and mounted smaller sieges. The comparative casualty figures between the garrison soldiers and those of the standing army suggest that there was little difference in terms of exposure to risk.

Bunyan's only comment on his army days has in itself puzzled many:

When I was a soldier, I, with others, were drawn out to go to

> *such a place to besiege it; but when I was just ready to go, one of the company desired to go in my room; to which, when I had consented, he took my place; and coming to the siege, as he stood sentinel, he was shot into the head with a musket bullet, and died.*

We are not told which town they were besieging when this incident occurred, and some misleading suggestions have been made that do not fit with known facts. A leading Bunyan scholar, Richard L. Greaves, has suggested that this event relates to the Siege of Oxford, one of Charles I's last remaining strongholds, in the middle of May 1645. It was a well-organised assault—a major operation. At Fairfax's request, 400 men from the Newport Pagnell garrison were requisitioned to assist in the siege. Fighting was fierce and many casualties were sustained before Fairfax decided to lift the siege on 3 June.

This scenario fits the description provided by Bunyan fairly accurately and also corresponds with the additional information given by an anonymous biographer in 1692. He reports that the 'town was vigorously defended by the King's forces against the Parliamentarians' and that the man who replaced Bunyan 'met his fate by a carbine shot from the wall.'

Another and more significant engagement soon occupied Fairfax and the New Model Army, accompanied by Cromwell . For at the Battle of Naseby on 14 June 1645, the Royalist armies were shattered, leaving Charles I so weakened that the defeat marked the beginning of a final victory for Parliament. Fought twenty-five miles north-west of Newport Pagnell, the battle was close enough to Sir Samuel Luke's garrison for him to supply arms and men if they had been needed. Services of thanksgiving to God after so notable a victory were held in many parts, and Sir Samuel Luke ordered a public thanksgiving at the parish church in Newport Pagnell.

However, Sir Samuel's days as governor of the Newport Pagnell garrison were coming to an end. A bill known as the Self-denying Ordinance had finally been

passed by the House of Lords on 3 April 1645, obliging members of the aristoc-
racy and of Parliament to resign their positions of command in the army or navy
in favour of men of military experience. Only by such a sweeping measure could
Parliament be sure that its commanders were single-minded and skilled in their
determination to prosecute the war. Captain Charles O'Doyley was Fairfax's
new appointment to be governor of Newport Pagnell. At the end of June 1645,
Sir Samuel relinquished his post.

We know little of Bunyan's activities for the next year. With the king's cause
rapidly disintegrating, military activity was scaled back. With the final fall of
Oxford in June 1646, the First Civil War was effectively over, and the king taken
into custody. Parliament ordered that the garrison at Newport Pagnell should
be dismantled and its fortifications removed. This would involve heavy physical
work and doubtless Bunyan was engaged in it. Some have suggested that he
then returned to Elstow, but this is unlikely for Parliament ordered that:

> ...all the officers and souldiers both Horse and Foot be forth-
> with employed in the service of Ireland... and it is further
> ordered that such common souldiers as shall refuse to go for
> Ireland shall be forthwith disbanded.

The fact that John Bunyan's name still appears on the army rota the following
year suggests that he opted to go to Ireland. Perhaps the adventure appealed to
him. More probably the lure of having his outstanding arrears of pay made up
was a further motivation. Following many delays and setbacks a small company, intended to be an advance guard, set off in October 1646 under Captain
Charles O'Hara and eventually reached Chester, where they were to await ship-
ping to Dublin. But after some time they learnt that units from the New Model
Army that were supposed to join O'Hara's men in Chester had refused to go to
Ireland until their arrears of pay were settled. In the end the whole project had
to be cancelled.

It may well have been while he was waiting in Chester on the Dee Estuary that

John 'fell into a creek in the sea and hardly escaped drowning', as he records in his autobiography. In later life he saw this incident as yet another of God's warnings to check his sinful ways. But, like the other near brushes with death, such a merciful providence appears to have had little effect upon him.

So with no alternative, O'Hara marched his men back to Newport Pagnell once more and here Bunyan's name appears yet again on the muster rolls for 17 June 1647 before he finally returned to Elstow.

CHAPTER 4

THE YOUNG BRAZIER

To return to the dreamy village of Elstow after almost three years in an army garrison — a melting pot of ideas, opinions and speculation — needed considerable adjustment for John Bunyan and could not have been easy. In view of his father's possible Royalist sympathies and the presence of his stepmother, it is unlikely that he would wish to return to the family home. But he probably had little option. He had a further year of a seven-year apprenticeship still to serve in order to gain his Statute of Apprentices. Not till then would he be qualified to set up as a brazier in his own right.

The only record that we have of the next few years of Bunyan's life comes from the pages of an account which he wrote more than fifteen years after the events. But as we turn the pages of *Grace Abounding to the Chief of Sinners*, we find few biographical details. No mention is made of his relationships with his family or friends, his home, his business hopes and endeavours—nothing. Clearly this was not Bunyan's intention when he wrote *Grace Abounding*—it is neither biography nor autobiography in the usual sense. Even the timescale of events which Bunyan mentions seems hopelessly tangled up and is impossible to reconcile with the known facts. 'The chronology is at best imprecise, at worst chaotic,' commented one historian. If we add up all Bunyan's references to periods of time in *Grace Abounding* it comes to about seven years, which must then be squeezed into the space of five years from 1651–1656. Certain events must therefore have overlapped each other.

But there are also enormous gains in this account. In a warm, dramatic, fast-moving story, Bunyan takes his readers with him from his early state of godless profanity to one of confusion, error and perplexity, and on to heights of spiritual joys. Then he allows us to crash down again with him into the depths of despair as he faces the fearsome attacks of Satan on his young faith. Yet always there is a steady, unerring progression towards his ultimate goal. This is a book with a purpose—it is intended to put warning signs along the path of Christian experience so that others may not stumble and therefore suffer as he did.

TROUBLED TIMES

But we must return to where we left John Bunyan as he finally received his papers decommissioning him from the Parliamentary army in July 1647. The war might be over, but there was little peace or stability in the country. The victorious New Model Army was becoming increasingly demanding and belligerent, particularly (and understandably) over its pay arrears. Authority was fast breaking down, with each man majoring on his own chosen agenda. The king, who had been in captivity since the summer of 1646, tried to take advantage of the situation. Then in November he made a cleverly planned escape from custody in Hampton Court Palace, absconding to the Isle of Wight. Recaptured on the island, he was held in Carisbrooke Castle. Despite this he began to negotiate with the Scots, promising to establish Presbyterianism for an experimental period of three years if they would raise an army on his behalf. Tempted by the King's terms, the Scottish army turned against its former Parliamentary colleagues and in April 1648 penetrated northern England. Carlisle and Berwick soon fell into Royalist hands once more.

Heartened by these victories, other defeated Royalist commanders rallied their troops and once more joined the fray with uprisings in Kent, Essex, Cornwall and Yorkshire. The Second Civil War had begun. Reacting with lightning speed, Sir Thomas Fairfax and Oliver Cromwell, together with the New Model Army, soon crushed the Royalist rebellion and once more tried to open negotiations with Charles I—a futile endeavour. The king prevaricated as before, rejecting any terms that compromised a full restoration of his royal prerogatives as he envisaged them.

Although John Bunyan would have followed the news of renewed fighting with concern, he was not recalled into active service in this further civil war, for he had never been part of the New Model Army. The country was now in a sorry state, the people frightened and troubled. Not only had thousands more died in renewed fighting, but trade was severely depressed. Continuous rain during the summer of 1648 had led to a disastrous harvest, forcing the price of wheat, barley and oats to unprecedented heights. Many poorer families were reduced to near starvation. No one knew what would be the outcome of these things.

Then in December 1648 came the series of events which led inexorably on to the final scenes of the life of Charles I, as he was tried and then executed in Whitehall Palace on 30 January 1649. As Oliver Cromwell gazed one dark night at the headless body of his one-time king lying in its coffin, he is reputed to have described it as a 'cruel necessity,' for Charles had repeatedly betrayed his own people. But many fell into a frenzy of misguided loyalty, comparing the king's death with the trial and crucifixion of Christ. John Bunyan too must have been troubled by these events, having fought for his country for almost three years. No one knew for certain what was going to happen next. Then in March Parliament abolished the monarchy and also the House of Lords. England was declared a Commonwealth.

MARRIAGE

While these momentous changes were taking place on the national scene, twenty-year-old John Bunyan had been making arrangements to begin working as a brazier in his own right. Now he wished to marry and settle down. Whether he had previously met and fallen in love with a Newport Pagnell girl, we do not know. Certainly his prospective bride, an upright girl from a good home, was not from Elstow, for there is no record of their marriage in the Elstow register.

It would seem that this young woman had been left in impoverished circumstances. Her father was dead, and probably her mother too. So there may have been no one to warn her of the enormous risk she was taking in marrying someone with a reputation like John's for wild and careless living. Describing his life at this time Bunyan tells us, that:

> *Christ found me one of the black sinners of the world, he*
> *found me making a sport of oaths and also of lies; and many a*
> *soul-poisoning meal did I make out of divers lusts as drinking,*
> *dancing, playing, pleasure with the wicked ones of the world.*

Beyond doubt John was deeply fond of his young wife, and in all probability the tall auburn-haired ex-soldier had swept Mary off her feet. Although John does not actually tell us his bride's name, we may assume it was Mary. The strongest clue is the prevailing custom of naming an eldest daughter after her mother, and we know that the Bunyans' first child was called Mary. And then there are the books. John tells us that his wife brought two books with her into her marriage—books that her father had given her. A copy of one of these, *The Plaine Man's Path-way to Heaven* by Arthur Dent had the name 'M Bunyan' in the front. Preserved until 1865, it was sadly destroyed in a fire at Sotheby's. A copy of the other, *The Practice of Piety* by Lewis Bayly, might also have once belonged to Bunyan's wife, as it has the initials M. B. in the front. Commenting on his marriage Bunyan tells us:

> *My mercy was to light upon a wife whose father was counted*
> *godly. This woman and I … came together as poor as poor*
> *might be, not having so much household stuff as a dish or spoon*
> *betwixt us both.*

But, poor as they were, they had at least secured a roof over their heads, a 'one hearth' cottage in Elstow High Street on the road to Bedford. Built of timber and plaster work with a workshop attached, it is generally supposed that John and Mary Bunyan set up home together there early in 1649.

Before long Mary was expecting her first baby and it was vital that John tried to extend his work as a brazier in order to support her. Day after day he tramped out to farms in the area with his tools strapped to his back — and a heavy burden they were, with his hammers, soldering iron and his anvil. Weighing sixty pounds, it was shaped like an enormous nail, with a flat head and a pointed end that could be hammered into the ground wherever he chose to work.

Bunyan's own anvil has survived. Discovered in 1905 among some scrap metal at St Neots in Huntingdon by a collector of odd or interesting items, it has the name *'J. BVNYAN'* in John's distinctive style of signature, carved on one side and on the other the old spelling of Elstow, *'HELSTOWE'*, with the date '1647'.

Sometimes John might be required to visit one of the stately homes in the area, and here and there we find traces of his activities. Tradition insists that he would visit such places as Houghton House on Ampthill Heights—still beautiful though now in ruins—to mend their pots and pans or undertake any other metal repair job. At Willington, five miles east of Bedford, is a strange old building known as King Henry's Stables, where Henry VIII is known to have stayed. The king's horses may indeed have been stabled there, but there is an upper floor used to accommodate members of the royal entourage. Soon after his marriage John Bunyan was called upon to do some work for the Gostwick family who now owned the property. Perhaps in some idle moment, he chiselled his name on the plasterwork over the fireplace on the upper floor over the stables, adding the date '1650'. The signature is still to be seen today, once again bearing John's own characteristic style.

A WIFE'S REPROOFS

More importantly, the year 1650 marked a significant change in John Bunyan's lifestyle. Shocked at her young husband's profanities and his careless attitudes, Mary frequently reprimanded him and told him anecdotes about her godly father, who would 'reprove and correct vice both in his own house and amongst his neighbours.' That was not all. She often reminded him of 'what a strict and holy life he (her father) lived in his day, both in word and deed'. Surprisingly enough, it appears that John accepted his wife's reproofs meekly, and does not seem to have resented her admonitions.

In addition the young couple began to read the books that Mary's father had given her. Described as 'a sermon on repentance', Arthur Dent's book *The Plaine Man's Pathway to Heaven* was first published in 1601 and had already gone through twenty-four editions. It sold over 100,000 copies before it began to lose its popularity. The book, a chunky volume measuring about six inches by three (15 by 7.5 cm.), consists of a conversation between Theologus, a divine, and Philagathus, an 'honest man'. They meet in a meadow one pleasant May afternoon and are soon joined by Asunetus, an 'ignorant' man, and Antilegon, described as 'a caviller'—a carping, critical type. A conversation lasting over 430 pages follows, as Dent uses the interchange between these characters to set out the truths of God's Word.

With sharp rebukes against sin and fearful threatenings against those who sin wilfully, Dent also holds out promises of the grace of God to those who repent. For John Bunyan these things came as a shock. He had spent years 'cursing and swearing and playing the madman' with little reproof. Now he learnt that these things were unacceptable to God. As he hammered away on his small anvil, the words of Arthur Dent would hammer away in his conscience:

> *Let not the wicked swearers and blasphemers therefore think*
> *that they shall always 'scape scot-free because God letteth them*
> *alone for a while and deferreth their punishment; for the longer*
> *God deferreth the more terrible will be his stroakes when they*
> *come.*

That was frightening. Not only did John and Mary read *The Plaine Man's Pathway to Heaven*, but also the other book Mary had brought with her, *The Practice of Piety*. Although the writer, Bayly himself, at one time the Bishop of Bangor, was not a very savoury character, his work is full of noble exhortations, a handbook for Christian living. The first effect of Mary's concern and of the books they were reading was to create in John the early awakenings of a desire to improve himself. Perhaps religion was the answer. It certainly had benefited his father-in-law. If he were to attend church regularly, not just on Sundays but twice a day together with the most devout of Elstow, that might satisfy his half-awakened conscience. He confesses:

> *I fell in very eagerly with the religion of the times; to wit, to go to church twice a day and that too with the foremost and there should very devoutly, both say and sing as others did, yet retaining my wicked life.*

FIRST MOVEMENTS OF A SOUL

The new vicar of Elstow, Christopher Hall, had been appointed by Archbishop Laud in 1639. Clearly semi-Catholic in his sympathies and practice, Hall's influence on John Bunyan in his present ignorance led to the young brazier falling under the spell of High Church ritual:

> *Because I knew no better ... I was so overrun with a spirit of superstition, that I adored, and that with great devotion, even all things, both the high place, priest, clerk, vestment, service and what else belonging to the church.*

Even worse than this, before long at the very sight of a priest had an intoxicating effect on Bunyan. He found that though the priest was:

> *never so sordid and debauched in his life, I should find my spirit fall under him, reverence him ... yea, I could have lain down at their feet, and have been trampled upon by them; their name, their garb, and work did so intoxicate and bewitch me.*

A dangerous condition in which to be, this strange fascination and delusion which gripped John Bunyan in the first movements of his soul towards God may well have been the origin of the legalism that would nearly destroy him in future days. Any exhortation from the vicar had a profound effect upon him. So it was that when he preached one Sunday on the evil of breaking the Sabbath day with 'labour, sports or otherwise', arrows of conviction shot through John's heart.

In 1633 Charles I had reissued *The Book of Sports*, first published under his father James I in 1618. Because the church calendar included so many 'holy days' as well as Sundays, the aim of this legislation was to allow the people, who normally laboured six days a week, to use leisure periods for various sports after they had attended the services. These included archery, wrestling, dancing, bowls and other games. And John Bunyan loved his sports. A strong, physically active young man, he entered enthusiastically into the rough games of football on the green and other such activities. But under Cromwell's new political administration, *The Book of Sports* was publicly burned and such sport prohibited. So when the vicar, who appears to have bent his convictions to suit whoever was in power, dealt with this very subject John first became aware of his own sinfulness:

> *Now I was, not withstanding my religion, one that took much delight in all manner of vice ... wherefore I fell in my conscience under his sermon, thinking and believing that he made that sermon on purpose to show me my evil doing, and at that time I felt what guilt was, though never before that I can remember; but then I was for the present greatly loaden therewith, and so went home when the sermon was ended, with a great burden upon my spirit.*

But it didn't last. While Mary was cooking him a good dinner, John began to forget his worries:

> *O how glad was I that this trouble was gone from me, and that the fire was put out, and that I might sin again without control! Wherefore when I had satisfied nature with my food, I shook the sermon out of my mind.*

It might seem that nothing had changed for the young brazier. But he would find that he could not shake off the secret workings of God's Holy Spirit as easily as he could the sermon he had just heard.

CHAPTER 5

A 'KIND OF DESPAIR'

I n a cheerful mood, John set off for the village green to enjoy a game of tipcat with his friends. Tipcat involved the player in first striking a small piece of wood, or 'cat', from a hole in the ground; as it rose into the air, he must strike it again. His success over his opponents was measured by the distance the 'cat' travelled. But John's game was interrupted that day. Nor was it merely the voice of conscience that arrested him: God intervened. Often referred to as the 'Vision on the Green', this event marks a heightened and new phase in God's dealings with this young man, and formed a significant turning point in John Bunyan's life. It is best told in his own graphic words:

> *But the same day, as I was in the midst of a game at cat, and having struck it one blow from the hole, just as I was about to strike it the second time, a voice did suddenly dart from heaven into my soul, which said, 'Wilt thou leave thy sins and go to heaven, or have thy sins and go to hell?' At this I was put to an exceeding maze; wherefore, leaving my cat upon the ground, I looked up to heaven, and was, as if I had, with the eyes of my understanding, seen the Lord Jesus looking down upon me, as being very hotly displeased with me, and as if he did severely threaten me with some grievous punishment for these and other my ungodly practices.*

This was not a vision in the usual sense of the word, for John tells us that it was 'as if I had ...seen the Lord Jesus looking down upon me,' but clearly it was a powerful and unexpected impression upon his mind. Again and again as we follow the tortuous path leading to Bunyan's eventual conversion, this pattern of sudden and surprising divine interventions is repeated, often happening in the middle of the normal activities of everyday life. Bunyan's reaction on this occasion is typical of his response at other times:

> *I had no sooner thus conceived in my mind, but suddenly this conclusion was fastened on my spirit … that I had been a great and grievous sinner, and that it was now too late for me to look after heaven; for Christ would not forgive me, nor pardon my transgressions.*

In one sense he was right—judged by the holiness of God, he had indeed been 'a great and grievous sinner'; but in another wrong—quite wrong. To presume that Christ could not or would not forgive his sins was a mistake that he constantly made and one that would haunt and hinder him in his spiritual quest. His conclusion, understandably, was now one of total despair. If he had sinned beyond forgiveness, he might as well go on sinning:

> *'I can but be damned, and if I must be so, I had as good be damned for many sins as to be damned for few.'*

None of those playing tipcat with John Bunyan that Sunday afternoon on Elstow Green realized what was taking place before their eyes. As John Bunyan resumed his game we can almost sense the bitterness of his despair. All the frustration of his present mood is packed into these words: 'I returned desperately to my sport again.' What more could I have done to attain the favour of God? he asked himself. I have reformed my life, attended services twice a day and venerated every object that was in any way connected with religion. And, if my heaven has already gone, then I had better blot out all thoughts of my irretrievable loss by taking my fill of sinning.

Whether John told Mary of the events on the Green that afternoon we do not know. But even if he did not, she could not have failed to notice the fearful change for the worse in his behaviour. In that critical moment he had decided to try out every sin, 'that I might taste the sweetness of it,' in case death should overtake him before he had found opportunity to sin to the full.

A GREAT SIN-BREEDER

If Bunyan's language had been appalling before, now every sentence was laced with oaths and blasphemies. Describing his condition, he later admitted ruefully:

> *I was one of these great sin-breeders; I infected all the youth of the town where I was born with all manner of youthful vanities. The neighbours counted me so; my practice proved me so.*

On Elstow Green he had managed to silence his conscience by assuming that all hope of salvation had gone. But though he went on in this manner 'with great greediness of mind', he soon discovered that more sinning did not silence his bruised conscience. Looking back, John Bunyan later commented that abject despair is often a stratagem of Satan to destroy a soul in its first steps towards God.

But God did not permit John to experiment with sin in so frightening a manner for much longer. And the means he chose to check him in his crazy course was totally unexpected:

> *As I was standing at a neighbour's shop window and there cursing and swearing, and playing the madman, after my wonted manner, there sat within the woman of the house, and heard me, who, though she was a very loose and ungodly wretch, yet protested that I swore and cursed at that most fearful rate, that she was made to tremble to hear me; and told me further, That I was the ungodliest fellow for swearing that ever she heard in all her life; and that I, by thus doing, was able to spoil all the youth in a whole town, if they came but in my company.*

Such a rebuke from such a person had a strange effect on Bunyan. For one who was 'a brisk talker', as John declared himself to be, we might have supposed that a torrent of self-justifications, or even a further flow of curses and swearing, might follow. Instead he reacted almost like a child before an irate headmaster:

> *At this reproof I was silenced and put to secret shame, and that too, as I thought, before the God of heaven; wherefore, while I stood there, and hanging down my head, I wished with all my heart that I might be a little child again, that my father might learn me to speak without this wicked way of swearing; for, thought I, I am so accustomed to it that it is in vain for me to think of a reformation, for I thought it could never be.*

However, against all John's own expectations, this incident, and the shame of the allegations made against him by one whose own reputation was far from savoury, brought about an amazing transformation. John Bunyan stopped swearing and astonished himself:

> *Whereas before I knew not how to speak unless I put an oath before and another behind, to make my words have authority, now I could, without it, speak better and with more pleasant-ness than ever I could before.*

But could this alone quieten John Bunyan's troubled conscience?

CHAPTER 6

'I PLEASED GOD AS WELL AS ANY MAN IN ENGLAND.'

Mary's first baby was almost due. With a deeply sensitive nature John longed to be a worthy father. Safely born on 20 July 1650, the young couple carried their infant daughter along the High Street to the parish church where John himself had been baptized almost twenty-two years earlier. Here the vicar baptized the little girl and, like her mother, she was given the name Mary.

After some weeks, like parents the world over, John and his wife began to look for those first smiles of recognition lighting up little Mary's eyes. But her eyes didn't seem to be focusing. Then the distressing truth gradually dawned: their baby was blind. 'Was this my fault,' thought John, 'a punishment for my sins?' Was this helpless infant to be condemned to life in a dark world? Undoubtedly with all his recent past so fresh in his mind, John would have made that connection. Their baby's vulnerability drew out a new seriousness and measure of tenderness in her father. Throughout her life this child would hold a special place in his affections.

John Bunyan had unusual musical gifts; one of his early endeavours after he left the army was to make himself a small metal violin—an unusual achievement—and on it he engraved his name and the name of his village as 'Helstow'. We can well imagine him sitting on a small stool in the evenings playing to his wife and to his infant.

A SECOND REFORMATION: PRIDE IN GODLINESS

John Bunyan still continued his efforts to improve, and this second reformation was more marked than the first. Earlier he had admitted, 'I was, notwithstanding my religion, one that took much delight in all manner of vice.' So now he set the Ten Commandments before him and tried to keep them. But this worthy endeavour was accompanied by a further fatal flaw in his understanding: he regarded a mere keeping of the law as *'my way to heaven'*—his passport to eternal life. And in his own estimation he managed to achieve his goal fairly satisfactorily. 'I … did keep them pretty well sometimes,' he recalled, 'and then I should have comfort,' and if he ever fell short and failed to obey one of the commandments as far as his own standards demanded, he would repent of his sin and promise God that he would do better next time. Having obtained forgiveness, as he assumed, he congratulated himself that he had 'pleased God as well as any man in England.'

And his neighbours thought so too. They took him to be 'a very godly man, a new and religious man.' Most were a little baffled at the remarkable change in John from a swearing, blaspheming good-for-nothing to an apparently upright and pious citizen. They 'did marvel much to see such a great and famous alteration in my life and manners.' John Bunyan managed to keep up this conduct for a year or more: and soon became a local wonder:

> *My neighbours were amazed at this my great conversion from prodigious profaneness to something like a moral life; and truly, so they well might; for this my conversion was as great as for Tom of Bedlam* (a nickname for any local delinquent or drunkard) *to become a sober man.*

Then the inevitable happened. People began to congratulate the young man on his religious life—a thing which pleased John Bunyan 'mighty well,' especially as it coincided with his own opinion of himself.

But to maintain such a standard was no easy task. Without the inward incentive of love to God and the help of the Holy Spirit, such ideals are irksome and displeasing to human nature. The driving motivation behind all Bunyan's endeavours now became his own reputation. 'I was proud of my godliness,' he confesses, 'and indeed, I did all I did either to be seen of, or to be well spoken of, by man.'

Mary's reaction to the transformation in her young husband is unknown. But if she compared him with her father, who appears to have been a genuinely godly man, she may well have seen through John's facade of religion. The path of the legalist and religious hypocrite is hard. Having produced an elaborate code of conduct, Bunyan was obliged to try to live up to the standards he had set for himself. Looking back later, he could see that he was nothing more than a 'poor painted hypocrite'. However, at the time he was quite satisfied.

While trying to keep God's law perfectly, another force was at work in Bunyan's mind: a growing sense of right and wrong. On Elstow Green he had managed to silence his conscience by assuming that all hope of salvation had gone. Now he made a further mistake by allowing his semi-enlightened conscience to become his dictator, distorting his rational judgement. The examples he gives in *Grace Abounding* to illustrate the effect of this borders on the ludicrous and may well have been deliberately included as a warning to others of the end result of such wrong thinking. Certainly it makes strange reading.

With his musical gifts, Bunyan enjoyed campanology or bell ringing. The belfry in Elstow stands separate from the main church and here Bunyan had a regular place pulling strenuously on one of the great ropes. But now, as he joined in this activity, a new thought suddenly struck him. Was it right for a 'religious' man to engage in bell-ringing on the Sabbath? Goaded by his conscience he forced himself to drop the practice. Instead he went into the steeple house and watched as the other ringers were at work pulling on the ropes.

Then another thought flashed across his mind: 'a religious man should not do this either.' The more John tried to suppress his conscience, the stronger became its repressive hold. Perhaps God would punish him: 'If I stand too near the bells a rope might break and a bell fall on my head.' Goaded by this fear he decided to shelter under the main beam of the belfry. There he would be safe, or so he reasoned. Then Bunyan's extraordinary imaginative powers took over—that same imagination that had led to his fearsome childhood dreams—a fresh thought occurred to him: 'If the bell falls it might hit the wall first and then rebound on me, killing me.' That possibility sent him scurrying to the door, where he decided he could watch in safety. Then a further wild imagination filled him with horror:

> How if the steeple itself should fall? And this thought, it may
> fall for aught I know, when I stood and looked on, did so
> continually shake my mind, that I durst not stand at the steeple
> door any longer, but was forced to flee, for fear the steeple
> should fall upon my head.

Many biographers and commentators on this period of John Bunyan's life have suggested that this episode reveals that he was suffering from an obsessive and unstable mental condition. If it is viewed merely as a psychological phenomenon, it is possible to understand such a conclusion, but this is surely faulty reasoning. This incident shows little more than the tricks an accusing conscience can play on a troubled mind. In addition, when he wrote *Grace Abounding to the Chief of Sinners*, Bunyan had a deep pastoral concern as his primary motivation. Addressing young converts whom he had in mind in this book, he writes:

> If you have sinned against light, if you are tempted to blas-
> pheme; if you are down in despair; if you think God fights
> against you; or if heaven is hid from your eyes, remember it was
> thus with your father, but out of them all the Lord delivered
> me.

A recent work on John Bunyan, refers to these incidents as 'the remorseless logic of the legalist', and points out what fearful conflicts a faulty understanding of the purpose of the law of God can produce on the mind and a sensitive conscience by forbidding things that are quite legitimate. These were in fact the opening rounds in that great struggle which Bunyan would face between his present wrong understanding of God's law, and of the grace which God provides in Christ—a conflict which would almost engulf him in the years that followed.

The next thing to go was his dancing, probably Morris dancing on Elstow Green. And this John found even harder to give up than the bell-ringing. But at last conscience won the day and he gave this up too: 'Now God must surely be pleased with him,' he reasoned. But far from condemning him, God was mindful of this young man's struggles and was about to intervene yet again in his life by preparing someone who would be equipped in an astonishing way to help John Bunyan—a man called John Gifford.

CHAPTER 7

WHAT THE TINKER OVERHEARD

John Gifford was a man with a story even more colourful than John Bunyan's own. Imprisoned in Maidstone, Kent, for his role in the Second Civil War, he was awaiting execution together with eleven other ringleaders. As a major in the Royalist army, he had taken part in a failed uprising in April 1648 in favour of Charles I, and now must pay the ultimate penalty.

When Gifford's sister arrived at the prison gates to say her last farewells to her brother, she discovered an astonishing thing. All the guards were slumped down at their posts, heavily asleep. Without anyone to question her right of entry, she slipped into the precincts of the town jail where another surprise awaited her. Contrary to habit, her brother had decided to remain sober that night, unlike the other eleven captured army officers who were all inebriated. Given such circumstances, escape became a viable option and, with his sister's help, John Gifford crept past the sleeping guards and out of the town, and hid at the bottom of a damp ditch. A massive hunt for the missing prisoner followed but after three days was called off. Gifford eventually made his way to Bedford.

A violent and godless man, the ex-prisoner was not subdued by his experiences. Taking up a position as a physician in Bedford, he soon squandered all his money at the gambling tables and on his excessive drinking habits. More than this, there was one man in Bedford whom he hated and wished to murder—this was an admirable and upright man by the name of Anthony Harrington. Why this should be so is unknown, unless it was because Gifford found Harrington's Puritan convictions and godly way of life an unbearable irritant. Night after night he planned his means of attack. Gifford soon learnt that his quarry was in the habit of meeting regularly with a few other like-minded men and women who studied the Scriptures together and shared God's dealing with their souls.

But before John Gifford could carry out his dastardly deed, God intervened. One night a particularly heavy loss at the gambling table caused him to curse God—a thing that even he had never dared to do before. Shocked at his own profanity, he hurried home and there picked up a religious book. The Puritan writer Robert Bolton was not one to deal lightly with sinners and his words crashed like thunderbolts on John Gifford's soul. His spiritual burden became intolerable, now outweighing all else. But where could he turn for help? Could God ever forgive so wicked a sinner? Then he remembered the small gathering of Christians who met together with Anthony Harrington. Perhaps they knew the answers.

Gifford's reputation had gone before him and, not surprisingly, the group did not welcome his visit and feared his motives. But Gifford would not be put off. His urgency to find the forgiveness of God was too intense for that. Each time they met, this unwanted visitor was present. And at last they realized that here was one who genuinely needed help. Before long John Gifford was a changed man by God's grace. Now all his energies were channelled into understanding God's Word and striving to please Christ.

A natural leader, Gifford soon began to urge the group, consisting of only four men and eight women, to form a church and establish regular services of worship. So in 1650, the very year that John and Mary Bunyan's blind daughter was born, this small group constituted themselves into an Independent church and elected one of their number to be their pastor, one who was proving an increasingly devoted and zealous Christian—none other than John Gifford himself.

John Bunyan knew little of these things, although perhaps the story of the astonishing change in the Bedford physician, a man called Gifford, had filtered through to Elstow, for Bedford had only a population of less than 2,000 at the time. Much of John's time was spent away from home, sometimes working in his clients' houses and often in distant villages in search of further work. Then he would roam the streets with the well-known tinker's cry:

> *Have you any work for a tinker?*
> *Have you any old bellows to mend?*

THE GODLY WOMEN OF BEDFORD

Little did John Bunyan think as he said goodbye to his wife and baby daughter one summer morning, striding out into the bright sunshine, that the day which lay ahead would be one of the most significant in his entire life. What happened next is best told in his own words:

> *Upon a day, the good providence of God did cast me to Bed-*
> *ford, to work on my calling; and in one of the streets of that*
> *town, I came where there were three or four poor women sitting*
> *at a door in the sun, and talking about the things of God; and*
> *being now willing to hear them discourse, I drew near to hear*
> *what they said, for I was now a brisk talker also myself in the*
> *matters of religion, but now I may say, I heard, but I under-*
> *stood not; for they were far above, out of my reach.*

We can imagine this young man passing along the street and suddenly catching a few scraps of a conversation that interested him. He stops, retraces his steps a little and with quickened interest stands nearby listening to the women who were sitting in the sun around the doorstep of one of their homes. Lace-making was an important industry in Bedford and probably these women had brought their work outside with them and while their fingers were deftly casting the bobbins back and forth they were deep in conversation. But this was no ordinary chatter, for their talk was about spiritual concerns.

Fancying himself quite an expert at religious talk, Bunyan thought he might even have an opportunity to contribute. But what he heard disturbed him profoundly:

> *Their talk was about a new birth, the work of God on their hearts, also how they were convinced of their miserable state by nature; they talked how God had visited their souls with his love in the Lord Jesus, and with what words and promises they had been refreshed, comforted, and supported against the temptations of the devil.*

The new birth? No thought of such a thing had ever crossed his mind before—he did not even know what they meant. Yet more strangely, they spoke of the wickedness of their own hearts. John had long since banished all such thoughts from his mind. Full of an inflated sense of his own goodness, he could scarcely credit what he was hearing: Satan's assaults, their own sins, failure and unbelief?

The articulate John Bunyan was now silent. Whether these women, members of John Gifford's new Independent church, were aware of the tall auburn-haired workman, his bag of tools on his back, standing within earshot, we do not know. Possibly they were so absorbed in conversation that they scarcely noticed him. Certainly they can have had no idea of the effect of their words on the bystander.

Not only was it their words that stirred Bunyan, but the way in which they were speaking. To John religion was a gloomy thing. Had it not taken from him all the things he most enjoyed in life—games on the green, dancing and bell-ringing? But these women seemed to know a joy to which he was a total stranger:

> *Methought they spake as if joy did make them speak; they spake with such pleasantness of Scripture language, and with such appearance of grace in all they said that they were to me as if they had found a new world.*

John Bunyan was shaken to the core of his being. He felt all his religious con-

fidence slipping away, all the duties in which he had placed his hopes turning
to dust:

> *At this I felt my own heart began to shake...for I saw that in*
> *all my thoughts about religion and salvation, the new birth did*
> *never enter into my mind, neither knew I the comfort of the*
> *Word and promise, nor the deceitfulness and treachery of my*
> *own wicked heart. As for secret thoughts, I took no notice of*
> *them; neither did I understand what Satan's temptations were,*
> *nor how they were to be withstood and resisted.*

Mesmerized, but also deeply troubled, the young brazier could hardly tear himself away, but when he did the words of these women, and their very tones,
rang constantly in his ears. In a few dramatic moments God had stripped from
John Bunyan all those attainments in which he had taken such pride. It was as
if he had everything to learn over again. Now he realized that he knew nothing
spiritually and, as he confesses, 'I was convinced that I wanted (i.e. lacked) the
true tokens of a truly godly man.'

What could he do? To whom could he turn for help? Drawn by an irresistible
desire to understand more of the joys which these women knew, Bunyan suc-
ceeding in organizing his day so that again and again he managed to be around
at the very time when the women of John Gifford's church were chatting together. Probably they were suspicious of him at first. Who could tell whether he
was spying on them? These were hard days for any who broke from the religious
mould of the established church. Disorder and confusion following the Civil
War and the execution of Charles I had led to the proliferation of various rad-
ical sects, increasing suspicion of any who did not conform to the Church of
England. But day after day it was the same. Whenever they took a break from
their work, snatching a few minutes to talk together, this same young man always seemed to be hovering around. Soon they learnt that he was a tinker who
had come into Bedford from nearby Elstow in the course of his work and that
his name was John Bunyan.

A CHANGED MAN

Two changes began to take place in Bunyan's thinking. First came a total re-assessment of himself. From being a self-congratulating religious hypocrite he now saw himself as 'a blind, ignorant, sordid and ungodly wretch.' But coupled with this, instead of despair as before, came a humility of mind which he describes as 'a very great softness and tenderness of heart which caused me to fall under the conviction of what by Scripture they (the women) asserted.'

Before long these members of the Bedford Meeting realized that the young man who so often seemed to loiter around was no idle, prying busybody, but a man deeply troubled about his own spiritual state. Gradually, as he grew more confident, John began to ask them questions—profound, perplexing questions—for now his whole being was taken up with one intense desire. Nothing, 'neither pleasures, nor profits, nor persuasions, nor threats' could quench his all-consuming hunger to know what these humble women knew. He had to force his thoughts to concentrate on his business and his daily life, for nothing else seemed to matter except 'eternity and… the kingdom of heaven.'

John Bunyan was indeed a different man. Many who read *Grace Abounding to the Chief of Sinners* puzzle over the question of when he was actually converted? Any number of points in time have been suggested, and any number could well be backed up by Scripture. And as Bunyan himself was to struggle over this very question in the months and years ahead, it is not wise to be dogmatic, but there are several fundamental things which strongly suggest that Bunyan was now a converted man. Who but a Christian would turn to God in dependent, self-effacing prayer in times of deep uncertainty and need? He tells us:

> *Unable to judge, I should betake myself to hearty prayer in this manner: O Lord, I am a fool, and not able to know the truth from error: Lord, leave me not to my own blindness… I lay my soul in this matter only at thy foot; let me not be deceived I humbly beseech thee.*

A yet stronger evidence is found in his changed attitude to the Bible. Now he read it constantly, recording that:

> *The Bible was precious to me in those days...I began to look into it with new eyes. I read as I never did before; and especially the epistles of the apostle Paul were sweet and pleasant to me; and indeed I was then never out of the Bible, either by reading or meditation; still crying out to God that I might know the truth, and way to heaven and glory.*

Summing up the mercies of God to him and the changes in his attitudes after his encounter with the women from Gifford's church, Bunyan he continues:

> *The Lord won over my heart to some desire after the means to hear the word and to grow a stranger to my old companions, and to accompany the people of God, together with giving of me many encouragements from several promises in the Scriptures.*

A long dark valley might lie ahead of this young believer, with many fierce battles against the enemy of souls, and much still to unlearn as well as to learn, but such evidences of spiritual thinking surely suggest that John Bunyan's feet were now planted on the rock of God's truth, even though he scarcely knew it himself.

CHAPTER 8

THE ROARING LION

To throw off a past of 'cursing and swearing and playing the madman' was no easy task for John Bunyan. A long and arduous struggle lay ahead of him in the months to come. Every scrap of his emotional and spiritual energy was engaged in the bitter conflict.

It seems as though that inner strife, with its advances and setbacks, was the only thing that mattered at this time. We look in vain for information about Mary's reaction to the change in her husband. Was her own religion anything more than an inherited code of practice learnt from her father in childhood? This and many other questions must remain unanswered.

We may wonder if Bunyan following the drama of political events unfolding in the country between 1651 and 1653. After all, he had fought with the Parliamentary army for almost three years. Did he know that the playboy son of the executed king had been crowned as Charles II by the Scots at Scone on 1 January 1651? Or had he heard of Oliver Cromwell's stunning victories over David Leslie and the Scottish armies, first at Dunbar in September 1650, and then of his 'crowning mercy' at the Battle of Worcester in September 1651? Did he wonder what had happened to Charles after this defeat? We may assume, however, that he would have known something of these great national events, but for the purposes of his autobiography all else took second place to that one momentous issue of his life: eternal joy or everlasting perdition.

The paramount question perplexing John Bunyan shortly after his first acquaintance with the members of John Gifford's Independent meeting was 'Whether I had any faith or no?' So untaught was he that he had to confess that he scarcely knew what the word 'faith' meant—yet he realized that it was an all-important qualification for any who would enter the kingdom of heaven. Yes, he was willing to confess that he was 'an ignorant sot, and that I wanted (i.e. lacked) those blessed gifts of knowledge and understanding that other good people have.' But did this mean that he had no faith?

He had not mentioned his problem to anyone and decided that perhaps the best thing to do was to put the matter to a practical test. We can imagine the troubled tinker trudging along one of the deeply rutted lanes not far from his home on his way to Bedford, his heavy anvil and other tools packed into a bag upon his back. Picking his way carefully around the rain-filled puddles, John suddenly had an idea.

> *'There is no way for me to know if I have faith, but by trying to work some miracle... I must say to the puddles "Be dry"; and to the dry places, "Be puddles". If a miracle takes place, with the puddles becoming dry and the dry places turning into puddles, then I will know for certain that I have faith; if nothing happens then I am surely a castaway and have no faith.'*

But just before he took the plunge a thought suddenly occurred to him: 'Go behind that hedge and first ask God to give me the power to do this miracle.' And God intervened yet again to prevent John Bunyan, not yet twenty-four years of age, from extinguishing the flickering light of true faith kindled in his soul. For when he emerged from behind the hedge he decided to wait a while before trying such an experiment.

At about this time John had a dream. Dreams had been highly significant in his life before now—as his childhood terrors demonstrate; but this dream was so vivid and detailed that he tells us that he could not be sure whether it was entirely a dream. In it he saw those joyful, contented women of Bedford basking in the sun on some beautiful mountainside. He, meanwhile, was shivering in the cold on the far side of a great wall that separated him from them. He longed to find a way through the wall in order to join them. Then he tells us:

> *I went to see if I could find some way or passage by which I*
> *might enter therein, but none could I find for some time. At the*
> *last I saw, as it were, a narrow gap like a little doorway in the*
> *wall, through which I attempted to pass; but the passage being*
> *very strait and narrow, I made many efforts to get in but all in*
> *vain.*

Although exhausted with trying, he managed it at last by lying on one side and forcing first his shoulders and then his whole body through the entrance:

> *Then was I exceeding glad and went and sat down in the midst*
> *of them and so was comforted with the light and heat of their*
> *sun.*

Bunyan had no difficulty in interpreting this dream. The mountain was clearly a symbol of the true church of Jesus Christ, while the wall was the words of Scripture which forbade anyone to enter except through Christ, the way to God. But despite his dream, the tinker was still troubled by anxieties. Not only did he fear that he might not possess true faith, but now another equally daunting anxiety distressed him: 'Am I one of the elect or not?' So much did this question perplex Bunyan that at times it seemed to sap even his physical strength. 'Though I was in a flame to find the way to heaven and to glory, and though nothing could beat me off from this, yet this question did so offend and discourage me.' Then an even more troubling thought occurred to him: What if 'the day of grace' is over and God has already chosen as many as he wants from these parts and I am too late?

In later years Bunyan would recognize that Satan was the source of these crippling thoughts and fears. However, at the time he tells us: 'By these things I was driven to my wits' end, not knowing what to say or how to answer these temptations.' Sometimes he felt like giving up altogether and collapsing beneath a burden of despair. But at the very moment when his thoughts reached a nadir of gloom, some words flashed into his mind from the pages of Scripture: 'Look at the generations of old and see; did ever any trust in the Lord and was put to shame.' 'These words ... were sweet words to me,' he tells us, 'for truly I thought that by them I saw that there was place enough in heaven for me.'

GROWING IN FAITH

Gradually John Bunyan was gaining ground, inch by painful inch towards that assurance of his part in the kingdom of Christ which he so longed to know. Comforted by Scripture, he would enjoy a period of calm in his mind, but then would be tormented by fears for Satan was not willing to lose this man without a struggle. If only he could *hear* a call from God, perhaps even with an audible voice!

> *'I cannot now express with what longings and breakings in my soul I cried to Christ to call me.' Gold! Could it have been gotten for gold, what could I have given for it! Had I had a whole world it had all gone ten thousand times over for this, that my soul might have been in a converted state!*

All this time John Bunyan had borne the burden of his anxieties and spiritual fears alone. But at last, and we may probably date this event early in 1653, perhaps eighteen months after he had first met the women of John Gifford's church, he plucked up courage to tell them of his desperate plight and his longings for a certainty of his acceptance with God. They in turn told their pastor about the young tinker from Elstow and all his doubts and desires.

John Gifford kindly invited Bunyan to his own home at St John's Rectory in Bedford. We may well picture the scene in that upstairs room where the two men met for even the fireplace around which they sat deep in earnest conversation can still be seen. Gifford was in every way the right man to help John Bunyan. He had sunk to far greater depths than the twenty-four-year-old tinker and had himself experienced the astonishing forgiveness of God for his past. Nothing that the younger John could say could shock or dismay him.

Sometimes the two might pace the rectory garden together as Gifford tried patiently and wisely to disentangle John's troubled thinking and point him to the clear teachings of Scripture. With a measure of surprise Bunyan records that Gifford 'was willing to be well persuaded of me.' Even after so short a time as a believer himself, Gifford could quickly recognize evidences of grace in others, and in the case of John Bunyan he had little difficulty in being 'well-persuaded,' even though John himself was so full of hesitancy and self-doubt.

The old legalism that had dominated Bunyan's thinking when he gave up his bell-ringing and other innocent amusements still burdened him. So fearful was he of disobeying God that he became enslaved by legal fears: 'I durst not take a pin or a stick though not so big as a straw,' lest it was stealing. A man who had once been 'a brisk talker' now feared even to open his mouth in case he sinned in his speech:

> *My conscience now was sore and would smart at every touch...*
> *Oh how gingerly did I then go in all I did or said! I found*
> *myself in a miry bog that shook if I did but stir.*

However, John Gifford's pastoral help, clearly evident at this time, begins to shine through in Bunyan's account of his life. Despite his fears, even he realized that he was now a true believer. Gradually he was learning that the only righteousness that would please God was to be found in Jesus Christ.

'BEHOLD THOU ART FAIR, MY LOVE, BEHOLD THOU ART FAIR.'

We may imagine John Bunyan joining the small congregation as he sat rather uncomfortably in the hard, tall-backed pews of St John's and listened with rapt attention to the sermons of his new pastor, Gifford. One sermon in particular stirred and comforted him. The text came from the Song of Solomon, chapter

4 verse 1: 'Behold thou art fair, my love, behold thou art fair.' The theme of the message was the love of Christ for his church: a love based not on any merit in the believer, but on the constancy of the character of God. Such a message was tailor-made for Bunyan's condition and was indelibly engraved on his mind.

Above all, it was just two words that affected him most deeply—the words, 'my love'. All the way home as he trudged back to Elstow they rang in his mind. Could Christ really love him in spite of all his sinning? 'Thou art my love, Thou art my love,' he repeated to himself over and over again, and now he added another promise from Scripture: '… and nothing shall separate thee from my love.' Such overwhelming joy flooded his spirit as he walked that he records:

> *I could not tell how to contain until I got home; I thought I could have spoken of his love and of his mercy to me, even to the very crows that sat upon the ploughed lands before me, had they been capable to have understood me.*

How great must have been Mary's surprise when she saw John's beaming face as he stooped to enter the doorway of their small cottage on Elstow High Street! She was now expecting her second child and was no doubt relieved to think that at last her husband had found that peace he had been seeking for so long.

CHAPTER 9

'GOLD IN MY TRUNK'

England in 1653 was far from peaceful. The Civil War might be over at last, but the aftermath of such a conflict, with its legacy of bereavements, anger and change, both social and political, was being felt throughout the land. Neighbours harboured deep suspicions of each other; vast tracts of countryside were scarred by battle; and poverty was widespread, with much of the cream of England's manhood dead on the battlefield.

The Parliaments governing the Commonwealth, set up by Oliver Cromwell after the execution of Charles I in 1649, were largely incompetent. By April 1653 the situation looked dire as members of the House of Commons wrangled ineffectually among themselves. Then Oliver's patience snapped. Without even waiting to change his clothes, he rushed to the House of Commons and after listening quietly to proceedings for a few minutes suddenly erupted into a passion of indignant oratory. Calling for his crack troop of musketeers who were already waiting outside, he forcibly ejected the Parliament and its members from the House. 'You have sat too long for the good you do,' he roared, and, in a final memorable act of intolerance, grabbed the mace from the table crying, 'Who will rid me of this bauble?' The only alternative remaining was to declare an end to the Commonwealth, and in December 1653 England was proclaimed a 'Protectorate' with Oliver Cromwell as Lord Protector.

Meanwhile, as we have seen, Bunyan's heart had been 'filled with comfort' as he mused on the sermon he had heard, and particularly on the words, 'Thou art my love.' It is likely that this was the period when he took the step of asking

John Gifford and the members of the church to consider him as an applicant for baptism by immersion—a courageous step in the mid-seventeenth century. Anyone who ventured to hold tenets of belief differing from those of the established church was regarded with suspicion. Bunyan himself does not mention the fact of his baptism, but a persistent tradition points to a small inlet in the River Ouse not far from the town bridge as the spot where he was baptized, probably at dead of night to avoid the ever-watchful eyes of those who might cause trouble. The site is marked with a plaque. Confirmation that his baptism indeed took place comes from a brief account of Bunyan's life written by a friend who knew him well.

THE BATTERING RAMS OF HELL

Shortly after his baptism John joined the membership of the Bedford Meeting; his name is found in the earliest list of members as number twenty-six. But, as so often happened in Bunyan's early experiences, this season of assurance and joy soon gave way to a further period of trial and testing. But this time he received a divine warning of the temptations that lay ahead. Christ's words to Simon Peter shortly before Peter's threefold denial of his Master kept ringing in his ears so clearly that sometimes he would turn involuntarily to see who was calling to him: 'Simon, Simon, behold Satan hath desired to have you' (Luke 22:31). Afterwards Bunyan could see that this was sent to prepare him for the coming onslaught of temptation, but he was so young in the faith that he could do little other than wonder about the strange phenomenon. Summing up this period, Bunyan wrote:

> *The Lord won over my heart to some desire... to hear the*
> *word... and to accompany the people of God, together with*
> *giving of me many sweet encouragements from several promises*
> *in the Scriptures.*

But then it seemed that Satan, with all the battering rams of hell, set to work to destroy John Bunyan's soul. The first temptation has a modern ring: 'How can I know that the Bible is true? Perhaps the Scriptures are all just myth and fable.' Then a yet more frightening thought gripped his mind:

> *'Perhaps there is no God after all, and no Christ. Perhaps the whole concept of salvation through Christ as a sacrifice for sin is one great deception.'*

Bombarded by such thoughts, Bunyan was given a practical proof of the truths he had embraced through a domestic situation that arose. It was the spring of 1654 and their second child was due soon—apprehensive days for the couple, particularly as their first child had been born blind. Then one night Mary appeared to go into premature labour. Panic-stricken, John didn't know what to do. With his wife lying beside him in bed crying out in pain, John began to pray urgently. If God would intervene and cause her pains to ease, giving her quiet sleep, then he would know that he was God indeed. Quite suddenly he became aware that Mary had stopped crying; in fact she had fallen asleep. And shortly afterwards John too fell asleep. Only in the morning did he think back on that experience and realise that God had acted to deliver him from the sceptical thoughts that were distressing him. But soon another temptation followed hotfoot upon this one:

> *While I was in this temptation I should often find my mind suddenly put upon it to curse and swear, or to speak some grievous thing against God, or Christ his Son, and of the Scriptures.*

The temptation to blaspheme was to Bunyan one of the most disturbing, particularly when he noticed that it was strongest when he was trying to worship, pray, or join in the Lord's Supper:

> *I could attend upon none of the ordinances of God but with sore and great affliction… Yea… uncleanness, blasphemies and despair would hold me as captive there.* 'Maybe I am a devil myself,' he thought morbidly, 'or at least devil-possessed. How

else could I have such horrible blasphemous thoughts when everyone around me is praising God?'

It is not surprising that Satan should attack Bunyan at so vulnerable a point, for as a youth he had indulged in fearful blasphemies, allowing them a place in his mind. Nor is this tactic of Satan a rare occurrence. Many other believers can also testify to such distressing temptations. In its most acute phase, it lasted the best part of a year for Bunyan, and yet there were moments of consolation as well, brief rays of light in the darkness. Sitting by his fireside one evening he was reading words from Hebrews 2. Suddenly the words brought such consolation and deliverance that he almost fainted, 'not with grief and trouble, but with solid joy and peace.' For he read of one who could 'destroy him that had the power of death, that is, the devil; and deliver them who through fear of death were all their lifetime subject to bondage'—even Christ himself. That John Bunyan should be reading and recollecting such Scriptures is in itself an evidence that he was profiting from John Gifford's ministry.

Although we are given so much detail about Bunyan's spiritual search, there is tantalizingly little information about his family life. As we have seen, John and Mary's second child was almost due. Their blind girl, Mary, was nearly four years old when her sister Elizabeth was safely born in April 1654, despite the scare a few weeks earlier. To the great relief and joy of her parents, this second child did not share the physical defects of her older sister. And for John himself, delivered for a short period from the tempter's fierce attacks, the safe birth of a second daughter was one further joy in his cup of blessings.

But as so happened often in Bunyan's account of these days, fierce temptations still assaulted his soul without warning bringing him into despair. Then again and again a word from the Bible seemed to flash into his mind bringing with it much-needed correction and consolation and balm to his wounded conscience. Words like 'This Scripture did most sweetly visit my soul,' seem sprinkled throughout his account. But the greatest deliverance of all came in another of those special interventions by God when Bunyan's conscience had become raw and damaged by the battering he had received. He tells us what happened.

> *As I was passing in the field, and that too with some dashes on my conscience ... suddenly this sentence fell upon my soul, 'Thy righteousness is in heaven' and I saw with the eyes of my soul Jesus Christ at God's right hand; there, I say, is my righteousness; so that wherever I was, or whatever I was a-doing, God could not say of me, He wants (lacks) my righteousness, for that was just before him. I also saw, moreover, that it was not my good frame of heart that made my righteousness better, nor yet my bad frame that made my righteousness worse; for my righteousness was Jesus Christ himself, the same yesterday and today for ever (Heb. 13:8).*

And it is with an exclamation of joy and relief that the reader also can greet the next words of this sorely tried young Christian:

> *Now did my chains fall from my legs indeed, I was loosed from my affliction and irons, my temptations also fled away; now also went I home rejoicing for the grace and love of God.*

'NOTHING BUT CHRIST BEFORE MY EYES'

The strength he now received as he finally grasped this vital truth did not drain away as he faced Satan's insinuations once more, and Bunyan's experience has brought relief to many others since his day. How gladly we read his next words: 'Oh, methought, Christ! Christ! there was nothing but Christ that was before my eyes.' As he quaintly put it, Bunyan now realized that he had 'gold in my trunk at home.' His treasure—his gold—was not his own goodness but Christ's perfect righteousness, freely imputed to him.

Not that his many trials and temptations suddenly came to an end, but they would never again master and crush him as before. But why, we may wonder, had it taken him so long to discover this? Why had he suffered such appalling temptations—temptations that have even caused some to doubt his sanity? As if he anticipates that his readers will be asking this very question, Bunyan pauses in his narrative to suggest some answers before proceeding with his autobiography.

First, he blamed himself. He had allowed a natural trait of character, his tendency to introspection and scepticism, to dominate his thinking—like Gideon, he had asked for signs from God and had not been prepared to cast himself on the bare word of the promises. But rather than dwell on his shortcomings, Bunyan preferred to speak of the advantages that he had gleaned from his experiences. Through them the character of God in his glory and holiness had been powerfully stamped upon his consciousness. Throughout all the trials of his future pathway those lessons learnt in the darkness would never leave him. Perhaps Bunyan's richest consolation and reward was found in all that he had learnt of the grace of God:

> *Great sins do draw out great grace; and where guilt is most terrible and fierce there the mercy of God in Christ... appears most high and mighty.*

Now and then in those early days after his deliverance from the tempter's clutches he was given such an indescribable disclosure of God's grace that he 'could hardly bear up under it, it was so out of measure amazing.' Indeed, this was yet more 'gold in his trunk'—a preparation both for the trials ahead and for the life-work which God purposed for him.

With new peace in his conscience, John Bunyan, now almost twenty-seven years of age, decided that the time had come for him to move his young family from Elstow into Bedford itself. St John's Church, the home of the Bedford Meeting, had become the central point of his life. He would naturally wish his children, with blind Mary now five years old, to come under the influence of John Gifford's preaching. Apart from this, his work as a brazier often involved him in visits to Stevington, some five miles north of Bedford. Sometimes he would need to go as far as Newport Pagnell to the west. If he moved into Bedford itself he would be more centrally placed to fulfil such calls. The Bunyans' new home was in St Cuthbert's Street, almost opposite the parish church. The cottage to which the family moved had two living rooms, one on either side of the front door, with a single room in the gabled roof where they would sleep. At the back, overlooking open countryside, was a small room which would later become John Bunyan's study.

In September 1655, not long after Bunyan and his family had settled into their new home, the Bedford church, and John in particular, suffered a grievous loss—one that must have seemed irreparable. That year, as summer turned to autumn, his pastor, John Gifford, sickened and died. None of the other members of the church had been able either to enter fully into Bunyan's trials or even to help him much. Although he was scarcely more than fifty years of age and had been a believer for only five years, Gifford had proved 'much for my stability', as Bunyan tells us. Doubtless the tinker from Bedford was amongst the few who stood around Gifford's bed as his life ebbed away. Perhaps he was also one of those favoured to hear the pastor's final words of passionate concern for the young church he was leaving behind. But now Gifford had gone, and John Bunyan missed him sorely.

With the loss of John Gifford's guidance and advice we may well suppose that this was the time when Bunyan felt most in need of a new helper—and he soon found such a friend—though in fact a literary one. 'I did greatly long,' he tells us, 'to see some ancient godly man's experience who had writ some hundreds of years before I was born.' Perhaps someone from a former generation who had gone through similar experiences to his own could be his instructor.

LEARNING FROM LUTHER

In days before much in the way of Christian biography was readily available, and when the cost of a printed book was virtually beyond the resources of a poor man, this must have seemed like a pipe dream. How his wish came to be fulfilled, he does not tell us apart from the simple facts:

> *Well, after many such longings in my mind, the God in whose hands are all our days and ways, did cast into my hand one day a book of Martin Luther; it was his comment on the Galatians—it also was so old that it was ready to fall piece from piece if I did but turn it over.*

Perhaps some bookseller gave it to him, because its condition made it virtually worthless. But, old and dilapidated though it was, to John Bunyan it was a treasure trove—more gold for his trunk. This book was everything that he had craved. All that Luther wrote rang true to Bunyan's own experience. Even the dedication in the first English edition caught his attention:

> *When I see a man (wrote Luther) that is bruised enough already, oppressed with the law, terrified with sin, and thirsting for comfort, it is time that I should remove out of his sight the law and active righteousness, and that I should set before him by the gospel... the promise made in Christ who came for the afflicted and for sinners.*

A misunderstanding of the purpose of the law given by Moses had almost crushed Luther and, in these worn pages which Bunyan now turned one by one, the great Reformer pointed to the same solution that Bunyan too had discovered when he had walked in the field that day and realized that 'it was not my good frame of heart that made my righteousness better, nor yet my bad frame that made my righteousness worse; for my righteousness was Jesus Christ himself.'

Bunyan's conclusion regarding Luther's commentary demonstrates the influence that this one book would have on all his future thinking and the comfort it brought him in his present condition:

I do prefer this book of Martin Luther upon the Galatians, excepting the Holy Bible, before all the books that ever I have seen, as most fit for a wounded conscience.

Indeed, John Bunyan now had a trunk full of gold, gold that Satan could no longer steal from him by his insidious temptations.

CHAPTER 10

CALLED TO PREACH

Coupled with John Bunyan's new and strong assurance of his salvation came an unusual sense that God had a unique purpose for his life. Bunyan himself was amazed at the strange inner conviction that he felt and which seemed to grow ever stronger. He records in typical Bunyan style:

> *Me thought I heard such a word in my heart as this—I have set thee down on purpose for I have something more than ordinary for thee to do; which made me the more marvel, saying, 'What, my Lord, such a poor wretch as I?'*

'Something more than ordinary for me to do'—what could these words mean? 'Have I understood them rightly?' he wondered. 'What about my weakness, my reputation for careless living in youth, my temptations, poverty, lack of education?' And yet the insistent voice in his heart kept on and on.

Although puzzled, Bunyan must have guessed at the nature of this special commission from God. For not long before his first pastor, John Gifford, died in September 1655, some of 'the most able for judgment and holiness of life' among the members of the Bedford Meeting had begun to notice John's extraordinary powers of speech and ability to express spiritual truth winsomely and persuasively. Realizing too something of the depth of his spiritual experiences, these people began to urge him to be willing to contribute now and then at one of their private gatherings.

Bunyan shrank from the thought. To him it seemed wrong that he should be placed in such a position, considering his recent and often continuing battles with fears and temptations. But his friends were insistent, and at last with much diffidence he attempted to speak a few words to a small group of fellow members of the Meeting. The result was astonishing:

> *They not only seemed to be, but did solemnly protest, as in the sight of the great God, they were both affected and comforted, and gave thanks to the Father of mercies for the grace bestowed upon me.*

Not surprisingly, the next suggestion was that John should accompany them as they went into the surrounding villages and that he should add a 'word of admonition' if the opportunity arose. Again Bunyan protested his inability, but again his friends prevailed upon him with the same result. Those who heard told of their joy at seeing what God had done in John's life, and urged him to continue. Gradually Bunyan himself began to sense an inward call from God and realized that God had indeed 'something more than ordinary' for him to do. 'I did evidently find in my mind a secret pricking forward thereto,' he tells us—not out of motives of self-aggrandizement or pride, for accompanying that 'secret pricking' was always a gnawing awareness of his own inadequacy, coupled with a constant harassment by Satan's fiery darts. But despite his fears he had a passion— almost a craving—to render to God his whole strength and any gifts he possessed.

A PREACHING TINKER

The Bedford Meeting members now numbered over ninety, a large increase on the twenty-five in membership when Bunyan had joined in 1653. Early in 1656 the church gathered with one purpose in mind: to set John Bunyan, together with several others, apart to preach. Not only was he to minister to the church, but also to preach the gospel among the unconverted as opportunities arose. This did not mean that he was to give up his daily employment as a brazier, but that he would accept preaching opportunities knowing that the church itself had the fullest confidence in him.

So whenever John Bunyan was able, after his long day's work mending pots and pans, he would trek out to some village, gather a congregation and preach. The results were astonishing. Often he could see the tears running down the faces of his hearers as his stirring words touched their hearts and consciences. At first he could hardly believe 'that God should speak by me to the heart of any man, still counting myself unworthy.' He tried to brush aside the evidences that his preaching was effectual and his hearers were being touched, but at last he 'began to conclude it might be so.'

What was John Bunyan's preaching like at this time? His vehement, burning words expressed the passion of his heart as he preached, although he later admitted that his emphasis on sin, the law of God and judgement to come without an equal emphasis on the grace and mercy of God, was inadequate but sprang in part from the anguish of spirit he himself had known:

> *I preached what I felt, what I smartingly did feel, even that under which my poor soul did groan and tremble to astonishment... I went myself in chains to preach to them in chains; and carried that fire in my own conscience that I persuaded them to beware of.*

To Bunyan's astonishment, and doubtless to that of the Bedford Meeting, he had not been preaching long before people flocked to hear him. Locals from Elstow came to see what had happened to John. Many, no doubt, had mixed motives for coming. We may assume that some came merely for the novelty of hearing a tinker 'prate', and others either to mock or wonder. Some, however, to John's amazement and joy, showed themselves to be 'so constant, and also in their hearts so earnestly pressing after the knowledge of Jesus Christ' that even he had to admit that God was owning his endeavours. As he saw the tears of conviction, penitence and joy streaming down the faces of his hearers, he realised, hesitantly at first, that these men and women were a solemn seal from God on his ministry.

For two years, so Bunyan tells us, the predominant note of his preaching was on the broken law of God and the fearful state of the unconverted. But gradually, as he himself gained a greater measure of peace in his own soul and Christ gave him 'many sweet discoveries of his blessed grace,' his emphasis shifted. He continued to preach what he 'saw and felt,' but now he 'did labour to hold forth Jesus Christ in all his offices, relations and benefits.'

As Bunyan's preaching centred more fully on Christ himself and on the certainties of salvation, he began to enjoy yet more liberty in preaching. Especially was this true when he was showing that our good works are not a prerequisite for God's favour—a lesson that he himself had struggled to learn. His description of such occasions is vivid and moving:

> *...it was as if an angel of God had stood by my back to encourage me. Oh, it hath been with such power and heavenly evidence upon my own soul... that I could not be contented with saying 'I believe and am sure;' methought I was more than sure.*

CHAPTER 11

DEFENDING THE FAITH

If we were to call unexpectedly at John and Mary Bunyan's small cottage in St Cuthbert's Street one evening in 1656, we might well be surprised at the scene that greeted us. In all probability Mary would be sitting nursing baby John, their third child, still only a few months old, while Elizabeth, not long turned two, might well be clamouring for her mother's attention. And there sitting at a table, making the most of the fading daylight, would be John Bunyan himself, surrounded by sheets of paper, with his blind child, Mary, nearly seven years old standing quietly by him.

To our surprise we would discover that the tinker of Bedford was writing his first book—a book designed to demonstrate the errors of the Quakers that were sweeping across the area at the time. Time was at a premium, for some of the most prominent citizens of Bedford had already been affected. Bunyan's quill scratched swiftly across his paper as all the convictions of his soul were poured into this treatise. Called *Some Gospel Truths Opened,* this book would run to approximately 40,000 words, mainly challenging the Quaker teaching that denied the true human nature of Christ. As Bunyan piles on the references showing Christ to be truly man as well as truly God, his exceptional grasp of Scripture is already in evidence.

Diligently and methodically, Bunyan worked through all the points where he felt the Quakers were in error, constantly emphasizing the real manhood of the Saviour in his virgin birth, his life, death, resurrection and ascension back into the glory. He laid particular emphasis on the return of Christ to judge the world, for his readers must be prepared for that great day—a day which, in common with many other Puritans, Bunyan considered to be imminent although he would not be drawn into the dangerous business of specifying times or dates.

Finally, John Bunyan puts down his quill. Perhaps he may read parts of it aloud to Mary, but all that now remains is for him to take his work to his new pastor, John Burton, and ask him if he will write a preface to it. He already knows of a London printer, John Wright, who will print his book, and an old friend from his Newport Pagnell days, Matthias Cowley, who will distribute the work.

John Burton read through Bunyan's work, touching up the spelling, for as we have seen, John had had little educational advantages. He himself was acutely aware of his lack of education and experience, describing his work as 'published for the good of God's chosen ones by that unworthy servant of Christ, John Bunyan of Bedford'. But Burton's final commendation of his younger friend and church member is warm and sincere, and bears testimony to the abundant blessing already attending Bunyan's preaching even as early as 1656. Burton could testify, together with many others, 'of this man's soundness in the faith, of his godly conversation (i.e. his way of life), and his ability to preach the gospel… and that with much success in the conversion of sinners.'

Soon after this John Bunyan was taken seriously ill. Not only had he been working throughout the day, walking long miles in all weathers with his heavy pack of tools on his back in order to earn enough to support his young family; he was also taking up every possible opportunity to preach in the surrounding villages. And now, in addition, he had written a long doctrinal treatise—an exacting task since it was his first—and had seen it through the press. Satan seemed to take full advantage of his weakness. Recalling this time, Bunyan wrote:

> *I find he (Satan) is much for assaulting the soul when it begins to approach towards the grave, then is his opportunity, labouring to hide from me my former experience of God's goodness; also setting before me the terrors of death and the judgment.*

But John did not succumb to such insinuations for long. Soon a verse of scripture 'did sweetly revive my spirit and help me to hope in God'—a passage from Luke 16 referring to the angels carrying the sick Lazarus to heaven. At that moment his darkness was dispelled and he cried out in triumph, 'O death, where is thy sting? O grave, where is thy victory?' As Bunyan slowly recovered strength, he was able to continue 'comfortable in my work for God again—a reference which shows how seriously he took his writing and preaching endeavours.

Shortly afterwards another 'great cloud of darkness' seemed to descend on Bunyan's spirit—a frequent after-effect of serious illness. Gloomy and depressed, he became acutely conscious of his spiritual apathy: 'I could not feel my soul to move or stir after grace and life by Christ.' We can well imagine him sitting brooding by the fire one winter's evening with Mary nearby, doubtless troubled that John should be so downcast again. Suddenly a verse flashed into his mind: 'I must go to Jesus.' Turning to Mary, he said, 'Wife, is there ever such a Scripture as "I must go to Jesus?"'

Poor Mary was mystified. 'I cannot tell,' she confessed at last.

Then it came to him. 'O now I know, I know!' he exclaimed elatedly. A passage in Hebrews 12 had sprung to mind: 'Ye are come unto Mount Zion, and to the city of the living God, the heavenly Jerusalem, and to an innumerable company of angels… *and to Jesus,* the mediator of the new covenant' (Hebrews 12:22-24). Joy flooded his soul. 'That was a good night to me, I never had but few better,' he records. All he longed for was an opportunity to share his ecstasy with 'a company of some of God's people.' 'Christ,' he declares 'was a precious Christ to my soul that night.' We can imagine him, some hours later, mounting the stairs to his loft bedroom where his children and Mary were already asleep. But there was little sleep for John: 'I could scarce lie in my bed for joy and peace and triumph through Christ.'

John Bunyan was entering on a period of great joy and usefulness in the service of the church of Jesus Christ.

CHAPTER 12

DARKENING SKIES

When John Bunyan published his first book, *Some Gospel Truths Opened* in 1656, England was still in a state of uncertainty and religious turmoil. These were 'distracted and dangerous times,' as he declared, times when many were 'tottering and shaking' because of the numerous religious sects that clamoured to obtain a hearing for their particular ideas.

If the religious scene was chaotic, the economic and political situation was equally confusing. After Cromwell had dismissed Parliament in December 1653, he had taken on sole rule, but was working towards the establishment of another Parliament. Convened at last in September 1655 and consisting of some 400 members as well as representatives from Ireland and Scotland, this Parliament also turned out to be a failure, unable to agree on a wide cross-section of issues. Exasperated and frustrated, Cromwell dismissed that Parliament as well in 1656.

It is unlikely that any system could have been made to work satisfactorily given the deep divide that existed between the aims and ambitions of the army and those of the gentry. Eventually Cromwell chose a highly selective Parliament to run the country, one that agreed with his own aims and ambitions—aims which he declared were for 'the healing and settling' of the nation. Because these were unnatural times, following a civil war which had torn the nation apart, such dictatorial policies were probably the only way to achieve any measure of stability. Fearful of renewed civil war in the event of Cromwell's death, the House of

Commons, actually offered the Crown itself to Cromwell in February 1657. He refused, although acting as king in all but name.

Persuaded as he was that Christ would soon return, Bunyan had little time to spare for other issues. As a preacher he must bend every nerve to stir up his generation to seek salvation before it was too late:

> *My great desire in my fulfilling my ministry was to get into the darkest places of the country, even amongst those people that were farthest off of profession... because my spirit leaned most after awakening and converting work.*

Many were ready to censure John Bunyan, particularly because of the focus of his early ministry on God's judgement against sin and the fearful results of rejecting his mercy. Much of this indignation, however, came from those who were either incensed at his doctrine, or who challenged the right of any layman, or 'mechanic' preacher to enter a pulpit. Bunyan tells us that:

> *When I went first to preach the word abroad (i.e. in the area around Bedford), the doctors and priests of the country did open (their mouths) wide against me. But I was persuaded of this, not to render railing for railing but to see how many... I could convince of their miserable state by the law.*

FIRST SIGNS OF PERSECUTION

In March 1658 a troubling situation arose while Bunyan was preaching at Eaton Socon, a village lying north-east of Bedford, not far from St Neots. Before he had finished preaching the local constable burst in demanding John's arrest for illegal preaching. Probably stirred up by the new vicar of the parish church, the constable had no actual right in law for such action, and so, issuing Bunyan with a warrant and ordering him to appear at the next assizes, he could only release him. The troubled church in Bedford gave itself to prayer 'for counsaile what to do with respect to the indictment against bro. Bunyan for preaching at Eaton'. As nothing more is known about the case, we may assume that the matter was dropped.

As John Bunyan rode further afield on his various preaching missions, he met with increasing opposition. In the village of Toft, five miles west of Cambridge, a friend invited him to come and preach in his barn. Towards the end of the sermon a Cambridge professor, Thomas Smith, arrived unexpectedly at the entrance to the barn. 'Who is this tinker, and what right has he to be preaching?' he demanded angrily. But when he heard Bunyan telling his hearers that he feared most of them were unbelievers and bound for hell, he was furious and accosting Bunyan at the end of the service demanded to know how he could describe a group of men and women, unknown to him personally and baptized as infants, as unbelievers? 'You lack charity,' Smith stormed, 'and are therefore unfit to preach.'

Without hesitation Bunyan told Smith that in those terms Christ's ministry too was 'uncharitable' for he often described religious people as unbelievers. Bunyan also had some provocative questions for Smith himself to answer: 'When were you converted, and what signs of new life accompanied that profession?' To be shown up by a mere tinker was more than the proud Cambridge don could bear, and he later published an open letter to the vicar at Toft, deriding the 'wandering preacher-tinker' and challenging his right to preach. 'What will be the sad consequences both to the souls and bodies and estates of you and your children in following such strangers?' he ranted.

Bunyan resolutely refrained from defending himself:

> *What shall I say to those that have thus bespattered me? Shall*
> *I threaten them? Shall I chide them? Shall I flatter them? Shall*
> *I entreat them to hold their tongues? No, not I! ... It belongs*
> *to my Christian profession to be vilified, slandered, reproached*
> *and reviled... I rejoice in reproaches for Christ's sake.*

Sometimes things went the other way. In another village, also not far from Cambridge, a Cambridge scholar noticed the crowds gathering in the churchyard. He wondered what the attraction could possibly be. Then he discovered that a tinker was to preach. Intrigued, he gave a boy two pence to hold his horse, declaring that 'he was resolved to hear the tinker prate.' But, instead of taking offence, the man was profoundly affected, converted and became one of Bunyan's most constant hearers, later becoming the minister of an Independent church himself.

Bunyan was not slow to recognize that behind the opposition he encountered was the power of evil. If God purposed to do a special work among the people, 'There the devil hath begun to roar in the hearts and by the mouths of his servants.' To Bunyan, therefore, the main agent of opposition was neither priest nor carping critic, but the Evil One himself. If he could not destroy Bunyan by one means, he would try another. The next stratagem he employed was to try to ruin his ministry by tempting him to pride on account of his outstanding gifts. 'I have... been often tempted to pride and liftings up of heart,' Bunyan confesses, but the strongest antidote he had discovered to this temptation was the continual sight of his heart by nature:

> *It hath been my every day's portion to be let into the evil of my own heart, and still made to see such a multitude of corruptions and infirmities therein.*

As we have seen, throughout this period Bunyan's preaching lacked a degree of balance, with the dominant theme being the broken law of God and the approaching day of judgement. This too became the subject of his third book, called *A Few Sighs from Hell, or The Groans of a Damned Soul.* Clearly the work was drawn from Bunyan's early sermons as two of his friends were later to explain:

> *His wit was sharp and quick, his memory tenacious, it being customary with him to commit his sermons to writing after he had preached them.*

A Few Sighs from Hell was from a sermon based on the parable of the rich man and Lazarus in Luke 16. An intense, terse piece of writing, packed with warnings of the fearful end of the unbeliever, it reminds us that Bunyan himself had not long emerged from under the shackles of a condemning conscience. He still remembered his fears as he felt the flames of hell licking around him. Such memories were imprinted indelibly on his mind, together with God's merciful intervention. As he told his readers:

> *When the law curses, when the devil tempts, when hell fire flames in my conscience, my sins with the guilt of them tearing of me, then is Christ revealed so sweetly to my poor soul through the promises.*

Bunyan was well aware of the impending storm that could engulf him as a lay preacher. Oliver Cromwell, by his resolute lead and firm grip on the nation's affairs, had given a considerable measure of toleration to Dissenters such as Baptists and Independents. If he should die unexpectedly the situation might change rapidly. And there were many ready to swoop down on a bold preacher like Bunyan and silence him forever. And he well knew that he could be among the first to pay a heavy price for his own staunch beliefs and his fearless declaration of them.

CHAPTER 13

THE STORM BREAKS

O n 30 August 1658 a violent storm broke over London, a storm of such magnitude that no one could remember one like it before. As crash after crash of thunder reverberated across the city and lightning split the skies in two, Oliver Cromwell, Lord Protector of England, lay dying.

1658 had been a year of personal distress for Cromwell. In February his youngest daughter's husband had died after only four months of marriage, but the grief that broke Oliver's spirit was the anguish of seeing the intense suffering of his favourite daughter, Elizabeth Claypole, as she succumbed to cancer, dying on 6 August. Worn down by long vigils as he spent wakeful nights at the sick woman's bedside, Cromwell himself fell ill with a fever, thought to be an attack of malaria. Soon it became evident that, although only fifty-nine years of age, he too was dying.

On 3 September, the anniversary of two of Cromwell's greatest victories in the Civil War, this fiery and godly man was taken from the scenes of earthly strife forever. But his loss plunged the country into a storm far greater than the one that had alarmed Londoners a few days earlier. He had not finally named his successor, and an envelope which he said contained the name of the man he had chosen could not be found. With the hereditary principle firmly embedded in the nation's psyche, Cromwell's elder son, Richard, was approached to succeed his father, though he was ill-equipped for such a charge.

JOY TURNED TO SORROW

While the people of England mourned or rejoiced, according to their political stance, over the passing of a great man, there was gladness for another reason in a small cottage in St Cuthbert's Street in Bedford. Mary Bunyan had given birth to her fourth baby, a second son whom they named Thomas. Their blind daughter Mary was now eight, Elizabeth was four and John two years old. But joy at the gift of this child was soon muted as it became evident that his mother was not regaining strength. Whether she fell prey to the dreaded childbirth fever, technically known as puerperal sepsis, a scourge which carried away many young mothers, we cannot know. Alternatively, in her weakened condition she may have succumbed to an infection such as smallpox or typhus fever, diseases which regularly swept through the community.

On the assumption that Mary was around nineteen or twenty when she married John in 1649, she can have been little more than twenty-eight when she died, leaving behind her young husband, scarcely turned thirty. For a man of such an emotional nature and depth of sensitivity, this loss must have been one of unimaginable pain for John Bunyan. In addition to his grief, his predicament was dire. How could he cope with four small children, one blind and another a baby of only a few weeks? And how could he support his family if he were confined to the house? Certainly his preaching would suffer. John draws a veil over his personal sorrow, but it is not hard to imagine how keenly he felt this bereavement. At such a time the closeness and compassion of fellow Christians in the church must have been an immeasurable consolation. It is likely that some of the women took it in turn to care for the bereft family and to nurture the newborn baby.

It may well have been during this period, when he was forced to limit his preaching and when his long treks mending pots and pans at far-flung farms had to be curtailed, that John Bunyan embarked on another book. *The Doctrine of Law and Grace Unfolded* would prove much longer than any he had attempted so far, and was one that marked a further milestone in his spiritual development. As Bunyan 'unfolds' the complex doctrine of the relationship between law and grace, the influence of Martin Luther's teaching in his *Commentary on the Epistle* to the *Galatians* is immediately evident—teaching which Bunyan had found 'most fit for a wounded conscience.'

Virtually all Bunyan's books were autobiographical to some degree. He had passed through deep waters both before and after his conversion and, out of the profundity of his own experiences as he wrestled his way through the problems of a misguided and confused conscience, he had many things with which to challenge and enrich his readers. *Law and Grace Unfolded* clearly reflects the liberating help Bunyan had received from the great Reformer.

For Bunyan, the law, while remaining a rule of life for the believer, has lost its power to condemn. Doubtless remembering the anguish of his own sufferings before he understood this, he exults in the liberating power of the covenant of grace:

> *Here thou mayest hear the biggest thunder crack that the law can give and yet be undaunted. Here thou mayest say, O law! thou mayest roar against sin, but thou canst not reach me; thou mayest curse and condemn, but not my soul, for I have a righteous Jesus, a holy Jesus, a soul-saving Jesus, and he hath delivered me from thy threats, from thy curses, from thy condemnations; I am out of thy reach, out of thy bounds, I am brought into another covenant.*

John Bunyan finds it impossible to write on this theme without constant recourse to his own traumatic experiences and the way of deliverance he had found for a distressed conscience. Whatever sin his readers may have committed, he assures them, there is infinite value in the blood of Christ, the cost price of that new covenant, to cleanse the conscience of the repentant. Perhaps the most moving passage in the whole book reflects Bunyan's own 'way of escape' from an accusing conscience:

> *Sometimes when my heart hath been hard, dead, slothful, blind and senseless, which indeed are sad frames for a poor Christian*

to be in, yet at such a time... hath the blood of Christ, the
precious blood of Christ... so softened, livened, quickened and
enlightened my soul, that truly, reader, I can say, O it makes
me wonder! Again, when I have been loaden with sin, and
pestered with several temptations, and in a very sad manner ...
I have found that when tears would not do, prayers would not
do, repentings and all other things could not reach my heart;
O then! one touch, one drop, one shining of the virtue of that
blood... hath in a very blessed manner delivered me, that it
makes me to marvel.

Although Bunyan was busy writing this important thesis, caring for his young family and earning what money he could for their support, he would also have been aware of the crucial changes taking place in the country—changes which would inevitably have serious repercussions for the small community of Christians in the Bedford church. And the nation itself was in a parlous condition. Following his father's death, Richard Cromwell had somewhat reluctantly accepted the responsibilities of the Protectorate. A country-loving gentleman, he was not cut out for the rough and tumble of political life. By force of character Oliver had kept conflicting elements in the army and Parliament in check. But his son was a very different personality and after little more than six months in office he resigned his position plunging the country once again into uncertainty and chaos. It was now effectively without any government at all, apart from a Committee of Safety, established by the army as an interim measure. Civil war once more loomed on the horizon.

A SECOND WIFE

As John Bunyan surveyed the chaotic political scene and the ever-growing possibility of persecution for any who dissented from the Church of England, he was deeply concerned for his motherless family. What would happen if he should be arrested and thrown into prison? There seemed only one solution: he must remarry. Encouraged by the church, John proposed to a woman by the name of

Elizabeth. Little is known of her apart from the fact that she was young - perhaps about twenty. There were several 'Elizabeths' on the membership roll of the church at this time. But of one thing we are certain: here was one of outstanding courage and faith. To take on a man like John Bunyan and his four children was also to share his sufferings, but Elizabeth rose to the challenge. It is likely that the marriage took place towards the end of 1659, almost a year after Mary Bunyan's death.

With his family once more under the care of a loving and capable woman, John was free to accept preaching engagements further afield. A number of north Bedfordshire towns were among those he visited towards the end of 1659. Sensing that his time might be short before his opponents succeeded in silencing him, he seized every possible opportunity to bring the message of the gospel to the people. The best recorded visit is of one he made to Yelden (now Yielden) on Christmas Day in 1659.

At Yielden a friend of his, William Dell, was the rector. A fiery man with deep convictions, Dell had been a soldier-chaplain in Cromwell's New Model Army. A strong tradition exists that he came to Newport Pagnell during Bunyan's army days and had a marked influence on Bunyan. Born in 1606, Dell was more than twenty years Bunyan's senior and now, at the age of fifty-three, was nearing the end of his ministry. But he was not popular with his parishioners at Yielden; in fact resentment had been building up against their rector for some time for the discipline he had been imposing on his congregation.

Then on Christmas Day, a day his parishioners regarded with particular veneration, who should climb the steep steps into the pulpit at Yielden but a mere tinker—one called John Bunyan from Bedford? This was one insult too many for the disgruntled people of Yielden, and before long they had composed a letter written to the recently reinstated House of Lords, setting out their multiple complaints. Dated 20 June 1660, the letter censured their minister, William Dell, on numerous counts. Among them was the affront they had endured when 'upon Christmas day last one Bunyan, a tinker, was countenanced and

suffered to speak in the pulpit to the congregation, and no orthodox minister did officiate in the church that day'. William Dell knew well that his days
among them were numbered.

And John Bunyan too was well aware that a storm might soon break over his
own head. How long he could continue preaching he did not know.

CHAPTER 14

'ONE HERE WILL CONSTANT BE'

S amuel Pepys, renowned diarist of the seventeenth century, was still on board *The Naseby,* flagship of the former Protector, Oliver Cromwell, as he sat writing up his diary for 25 May 1660. *The Naseby,* named to commemorate Parliament's important victory over the Royalists in 1645, had been hastily redecorated to remove all evidences of its past usage. For none other than Charles, son of the beheaded previous king, was on board, returning to England from Holland by popular demand of the people.

As England had spiralled into chaos following the resignation of Richard Cromwell, the prospect of renewed civil war following the collapse of the Protectorate was real. General Monck who had served under Cromwell as commander-in-chief in Scotland, marched south on 1 January with an army at his back. Everywhere he went he discovered the people were fearful and longing for nothing more than stability, even if it meant a return of the Stuarts. Monck set up another Parliament and a call was issued to the son of the executed Charles I to return from exile in France and accept the crown of England. Charles then drew up what has become known as the *Declaration of Breda* in which he set out his terms for accepting the Crown.

Although it appears that no conditions were laid down for him to fulfil before he would be welcomed, he undertook to grant a 'free and general pardon' to any old enemies as long as they would recognize him as king. Above all, and most importantly for John Bunyan, he promised 'liberty for tender consciences' over matters of religion. But the new Parliament, made up largely of Royalists with old scores to settle, determined to restore the status of the Church of England as the national church and the office of bishops which had been in abeyance. No longer must laymen like John Bunyan occupy a pulpit. The *Book of Common Prayer* was reintroduced with bishops and clergy who had been excluded from their former churches flocking back to take up their positions again.

INCREASING DANGER

The Bedford Meeting to which Bunyan belonged quickly felt the impact of such changes. By June 1660, scarcely a month after Charles had arrived back on English shores, the church was turned out of St John's, the parish church where it had been meeting for the last seven years. The previous rector, Theodore Crowley, dismissed from the living in 1653 because of his opposition to Puritanism, now came back to claim it. Nor was this their only problem. For the church was leaderless once more, as their pastor, John Burton, who had followed John Gifford had just died.

John Bunyan was well aware of the ever-increasing dangers that surrounded him as he set out on his preaching engagements. His enemies were ready to pounce although no law had as yet been passed forbidding private gatherings for spiritual worship. The minute book of the Bedford Meeting reflects the growing concerns of Independent churches at this time and sought a closer co-operation with other likeminded groups in order that they might all stand together in adversity.

When John Bunyan set out for Lower Samsell, near Harlington, some twelve miles south of Bedford, on 12 November 1660, he knew that he was under surveillance. It must have been with a heavy heart that he said an affectionate goodbye to Elizabeth and the children. Would he come home safely? He did not know. Each time he ventured out to preach he took a serious risk. Silently his 'congregation' slipped across the fields to the isolated farmstead. As John Bunyan stabled his horse and entered, the farmer took him aside and whispered urgently in his ear of rumours he had heard of a warrant issued for John's arrest. Surely it would be better to disband the meeting and play safe.

Not only had the local magistrate Francis Wingate issued such a warrant, but he had also ordered that a close watch be kept on the property, fearing that those who met there might be plotting some dastardly plan to overthrow the new government. Possibly knowing more than Bunyan did about Wingate's unsavoury character and his determination to bully Dissenters into submission, the farmer was seriously alarmed both for the preacher and the people. But Bunyan was resolute, replying:

> No, l will not stir, neither will I have the meeting dismissed for this. Come, be of good cheer, let us not be daunted; our cause is good, we need not be ashamed of it; to preach God's word is so good a work that we shall be well rewarded if we suffer for that.

But clearly the farmer's fears were felt by all present. Perhaps, thought Bunyan, I ought to reconsider my decision and step outside and give the matter more prayer. Maybe the thought of Elizabeth and the children flashed across his mind. Elizabeth was pregnant with her first child. How she needed him at such a time! Could she possibly cope with five young children all under the age of ten if he were imprisoned? But, on the other hand, what damage it would do to the gospel cause for which he stood if he should weaken! Gradually, as he paced among the elm trees surrounding the farm, a quiet determination gripped him. Perhaps some words of Nehemiah rang in his mind: 'Should such a man as I flee?' Or, as Bunyan put it:

> I walked into the close where… this came into my mind, That I had showed myself hearty and courageous in my preaching… and thought I, if I should now run and make an escape, it will be of very ill savour in the country. For what will my weak

and newly converted brethren think of it, but that I was not so strong in deed as I was in word.

No, he must stand firm, come what may. If he should weaken, opponents would take the opportunity to mock the gospel, and with it the truths that he had preached—and that, he determined, must never be.

FIRST ARREST

Returning to the house, Bunyan opened the meeting. We can well imagine with what earnestness he prayed for strength to endure the trials that might come. He had not been speaking for long before a rude hammering at the door alerted the worshippers to the fact that their worst fears had indeed been realized. The local constable, together with Wingate's representative, burst in demanding the immediate arrest of John Bunyan. Although instructed to accompany them without delay, John Bunyan was in no hurry. First, he insisted, he must address his distressed hearers assuring them that 'we suffer as Christians for well doing: and we had better be the persecuted than the persecutors.'

Scarcely able to contain their impatience, the constable and Wingate's man kept interrupting while Bunyan tried to comfort those meeting with him. At last they moved off into the darkness of the November night, with Bunyan between them. Doubtless someone else hurried to Bedford to bring Elizabeth the grievous news that John was under arrest.

Closely guarded at a friend's house overnight, Bunyan was conducted to Harlington Manor in the morning where Francis Wingate was waiting, seated behind a table. Also born in 1628, only a few weeks before Bunyan, Wingate eyed the young preacher carefully before questioning him. Appointed as a Justice of the Peace, with a brief to keep the peace in his area, Wingate acted as judge and jury in one. He was a convinced Royalist and his family had suffered some loss of property in the Civil War. Certainly he had no love for Puritans, least of all for John Bunyan, whom he had long regarded as a troublemaker, particularly on his preaching visits to Lower Samsell, an area which fell within Wingate's jurisdiction.

But first Wingate had to ask a few questions of the constable who had arrested Bunyan. Perhaps Bunyan and those with him at the farm were up to no good, perhaps even planning some sort of insurrection to overthrow the new and still vulnerable regime. He fired his questions like bullets. 'How many were there? What were they doing? What did they have with them? Were they armed?' Far from uncovering some anti-government plot, the constable admitted that he had found only a few men and women gathered together to attend the preaching of God's word.

Abashed, Francis Wingate scarcely knew how to proceed. He had ordered the arrest of this man, but what accusations could he level at him? Swiftly changing course, he began questioning Bunyan about an issue where the young tinker-preacher was indeed vulnerable. 'What were you doing there,' he demanded, 'and why can you not be contented with following your proper calling? Do you not know that it is against the law for such as you to be preaching?'

Not to be beaten, Bunyan countered firmly:

> *The intent of my coming thither (to Lower Samsell) and to other places was to instruct and counsel people to forsake their sins, and close in with Christ, lest they perish miserably.*

Wingate coloured up with rage. Bunyan had touched on the very issue that maddened him. 'I will break the neck of your meetings,' he threatened angrily. 'It might be so,' was Bunyan's simple reply.

Without further ado, Wingate ordered Bunyan to arrange for men who would stand surety for him; otherwise he must go straight to prison. Although Bunyan had friends ready to support him, Wingate stipulated that they must bind themselves to prevent Bunyan from preaching. It was useless. With great courage and dignity, Bunyan released his friends from any such commitment declaring that nothing would stop him and insisting:

> *I should not leave speaking the Word of God even to counsel,*
> *comfort, exhort and teach the people among whom I came,*
> *and I thought this to be a work that had no hurt in it; but was*
> *rather worthy of commendation than blame.*

Infuriated at the calm boldness of the man in front of him, Wingate announced harshly that a legal warrant was to be prepared immediately, committing Bunyan to the County Jail. Here he would remain until the next quarter-sessions when cases came up for trial before the circuit magistrates.

Bunyan had deliberately chosen a path of obedience to God, cost what it might in earthly terms. It was even as he would later write:

> *Who would true valour see*
> *let him come hither.*
> *One here will constant be*
> *come wind, come weather.*

CHAPTER 15

BY THE LIGHT OF A CANDLE

Harlington parish church of St Mary the Virgin, built in the thirteenth century, was no more than a minute's walk from Harlington Manor. Nearby stood the vicarage, home of Dr Lindall, who had served as vicar in the village for seventeen years. He kept a close watch on all the activities in the community; if anything unusual was afoot at the Manor House, Dr Lindall was sure to hear about it. So for him to arrive on the scene where Bunyan was being interrogated was not surprising. He had probably been glad to hear of the arrest of that tinker who went about preaching in his and other men's parishes, and who was nothing but a worthless nuisance in his eyes.

As John Bunyan stood waiting for the warrant for his imprisonment to be drawn up, Dr Lindall entered the parlour. Bunyan recognized him instantly, undoubtedly he had had previous experience of this man for Lindall 'fell to taunting at me in many reviling terms.' Ignoring the insults, Bunyan merely replied that his business was with the magistrate, not with the vicar. When Lindall found that he could not provoke Bunyan into an argument, he began to heap further abuse on the prisoner, jeering at his predicament. What right had a tinker to be preaching anyway? The sneers were not lost on Bunyan.. Without a moment's hesitation he had his answer ready: 'I also have read of very many priests and Pharisees that had their hands in the blood of the Lord Jesus Christ.'

Doubtless Bunyan felt a measure of relief when Wingate reappeared with the warrant in his hand. Stating that the accused 'went about to several conventicles (or small gatherings) in the country to the great disparagement of the Church of England,' the warrant ordered that he must remain in prison unless he could find sureties who would stand bail for him until the next assizes, when his case would be heard by the county magistrates.

A FALSE HOPE

At last the end of this grievous day was approaching. But Bunyan and the constable had no sooner left the Manor House to begin the long walk to Bedford Jail before two of Bunyan's friends came hurrying up, begging the constable to wait. Deeply troubled that a man like Bunyan should be thrown into prison, these men had been taking advice, probably from a lawyer, to see if anything could be done to secure the preacher's release. And now they urgently begged for an opportunity to speak to the magistrate.

Full of hope, his friends hurried in to where Francis Wingate still remained seated in order to press their case. The short November day was drawing to a close and darkness now enveloped the scene as Bunyan wearily followed them back to the house. Doubtful that any expedient could prevail, he felt that he must at least attempt to co-operate with such well-intentioned friends. But at the same time he tells us that:

> *I lifted up my heart to God for light and strength to be kept,*
> *that I might not do anything that might either dishonour him*
> *or wrong my own soul or be a grief or discouragement to any*
> *that was inclining after the Lord Jesus Christ.*

Before long his friends were back, bright with optimism. Bunyan listened while they explained that they had been advised that all he had to do was to say 'certain words' and he could be set free. Realizing their kindly motives, Bunyan could only ask, 'What words are these?' but added that if the words were 'such that might be said with a good conscience' he would say them; otherwise he would not.

Then Bunyan noticed another door gradually opening. Someone was entering the room with a lighted candle in one hand. As the newcomer was standing in the shadows, Bunyan may not have recognized him immediately, but as the uplifted candle cast its flickering light across the man's face, he knew who it was—none other than a lawyer by the name of William Foster, one who 'had ever been a close opposer of the ways of God.'

'Who is there? John Bunyan?' cried the stranger in mock surprise. Placing his candle on a table, Foster hurried towards the prisoner, arms stretched out as though to embrace him like a long-lost friend. Bunyan records that it seemed 'as if he would have leaped on my neck and kissed me.' Such a show of unexpected affection did not fool Bunyan. 'Beware of men', he thought, recollecting the Saviour's words, and later another verse of Scripture flashed through his mind: 'Their tongues are smoother than oil. But their words are drawn swords.'

'Blessed be God, I am well,' answered John cautiously in response to Foster's exuberant greeting.

'What is the occasion of your being here?' asked Foster, already knowing the answer full well.

'I was at a meeting of people a little way off, intending to speak a word of exhortation to them, but the Justice, hearing thereof was pleased to send his warrant to fetch me here before him,' replied Bunyan.

'So I understand,' Foster answered. Then, clearly being privy to the 'certain words' that Bunyan must speak to secure his liberty, he continued: 'If you will promise to call people no more together, you shall have your liberty to go home, for my brother (Wingate) is very loath to send you to prison, if you will be but ruled.'

'What do you mean by "not calling the people together"?' Bunyan enquired, explaining that his only purpose at any gathering of people was to 'exhort and counsel them to seek after the Lord Jesus Christ for the salvation of their souls.'

'Only say that you will not call people together,' Foster insisted.

Bunyan was astute enough to know that this was nothing but a trap to stop him from preaching. Realizing that the tinker was not going to be so easily hoodwinked, Foster came directly to the point. Preaching, he growled, was none of Bunyan's business. All he must do was to leave off his preaching and to follow his normal vocation.

But Bunyan was immovable. 'I can follow my calling and preach the Word,' he retorted, 'and it is my duty to do them both as long as I have opportunity.'

At this point all Foster's assumed pleasantries evaporated and, like Dr Lindall, he too became abusive, accusing Bunyan of being exactly like the 'papists'. Back and forth went the arguments, as Bunyan had an answer for everything that Foster could throw at him. At last Foster came full circle back to the 'words' Bunyan must say in order to be released. If only he would promise never to gather a congregation he would be free. 'But,' protested Bunyan, 'if people choose to come together when I speak, I cannot be held responsible for that.' Certainly he could make no such commitment.

At last he told Foster, 'I dare say no more than I have said, for I dare not leave off that work to which God has called me.'

Outflanked by a mere tinker, Foster picked up his candle and left the room, clearly intending to advise Wingate on how he should proceed in this case. Alone in the dark, Bunyan foresaw the outcome exactly. And as he anticipated, Foster advised that the only course was to send the obstinate tinker to prison, because it was obvious that he would not see reason. As Bunyan records, 'The man that did at the first express so much love to me, told the Justice that he must send me away to prison.'

It was now too late to walk the thirteen miles from Harlington to Bedford, and a strong tradition remains that he was ushered into an attic room in the Manor House to spend the night. it is not hard to imagine the thoughts that raced through his mind during the long dark hours. How could he face the coming weeks of confinement? How could he provide for his family? Somehow he must prepare his spirit for whatever eventuality might transpire. Perhaps the only way was to anticipate the very worst situation possible —even the imposition of the death sentence—so that no degree of suffering could find him unprepared.

PEACE IN THE STORM

Whatever the thoughts that crowded Bunyan's mind that night, as morning broke, he must prepare for the long walk to Bedford Jail and an unknown future. But by this time God had given his faithful servant so marked a degree of inward peace that he could hardly stop himself from telling his scheming adversaries about it. As he later wrote, 'I carried the peace of God along with me… and, blessed be the Lord, went away to prison with God's comfort in my poor soul.'

Bunyan still had much to occupy his thoughts as he tramped along the muddy roads with the constable at his side. He must have wondered time and again about Elizabeth and the children. He had been away from home for two nights. Did Elizabeth know where he was? She was so young. How were these things affecting her? With her baby so nearly due, John longed to go to her. In spite of his sense of peace, he still had many fears:

> *Before I came to prison I saw what was a-coming, and had
> especially two considerations warm upon my heart; the first
> was how to be able to endure should my imprisonment be long
> and tedious; the second was how to be able to encounter death,
> should that be here my portion.*

Such thinking was not new to him. For almost a year he had anticipated this eventuality as he had seen the mounting opposition to his preaching. Several verses of Scripture had been of special consolation and had prepared him for the suffering that might lie ahead. One particularly was 'of great use'. The apostle Paul says, 'We had the sentence of death in ourselves that we should not trust in ourselves, but in God who raises the dead' (2 Corinthians 1:9). Yes, Bunyan knew that he too must place all that he held dear under a 'sentence of death', for, as he expressed it:

> *If ever I would suffer rightly I must first pass a sentence of death upon everything that can properly be called a thing of this life, even to reckon myself, my wife, my children, my health, my enjoyments, and all as dead to me and myself as dead to them. The second was to live upon God that is invisible.*

CHAPTER 16

A PRISONER OF CONSCIENCE

Bedford County Jail stood grim and forbidding on that bleak November morning in 1660. All that now remains of the old prison, demolished in 1802, are two of its gates that once opened onto the street. Constructed of oak and heavily studded, both have bars across a central aperture or grate. Here prisoners would stand and beg for gifts of food or money from passers-by, or they might attempt to sell products they had made in the prison in order to support their families.

Calling for the jailer, the constable explained the reason for the new prisoner's arrest and handed over the warrant signed by Francis Wingate. Before many moments had passed John Bunyan was thrust into the prison, the ominous-looking gate closing behind him with a resounding thud. Although no pictures have survived of the former County Jail, John Howard (1726–1790), a notable eighteenth-century prison reformer, also from Bedford, has left a description of it in his monumental work, *The State of the Prisons in England and Wales*. Writing over a century after Bunyan's imprisonment, he describes the two-storeyed building and its dungeons below street level. On the ground floor were two day-rooms, each about eight feet square, one for men and the other for women. These were set aside for criminals: murderers, thieves, pickpockets, cheats and others guilty of various acts of felony. The rooms were small, for most inmates were only short-stay prisoners, soon being led away to be hung. Opening off the day rooms were two cells, called lodging rooms, one each for men and women, where prisoners slept at night, often in chains. Down eleven slippery steps were the dungeons, reserved for any prisoner who had proved awkward in some way.

One had a small skylight, but both were dark, dank and airless—terrible places where men were often left to die.

On the upper floor was the debtors' day room, larger than the felons' quarters, and one which sometimes doubled as a chapel. Leading off from this were four lodging rooms for sleeping quarters. Nothing but straw was supplied for prisoners to lie on at night, and this had to be paid for by the prisoner. If he were too poor to buy straw, mere rags might do for bedding, or alternatively, scraps of straw left over from men and women already executed. No form of heating was provided and when temperatures dropped dramatically during the winter months many prisoners would contract serious diseases or die.

To this upper floor the new prisoner was now escorted. Furnishings were scant, and Bunyan's fellow prisoners were among the poorest in the community, many thrown into prison because of unpaid debts. Some indeed were rascals, penniless because of their own misconduct, but most were those whose lot in life had brought them and their families to the brink of starvation. Conditions for debtors could be appalling. Describing them a hundred years later, John Howard writes of men and women 'expiring on the floors in loathsome cells, sometimes in two or three inches of effluence.' We cannot imagine Bunyan's circumstances to have been much better, although it is known that his first jailer was more humane than most.

LIFE IN PRISON

Prisoners were expected to pay the jailer for their rations of food, or else they must rely on gifts brought to the jail by family members or friends. Lack of food brings out the worst in people, and when the jailer distributed the 'pennyworth of bread' or 'the two quarter loaves a week' allocated to each prisoner, the sick and friendless could easily find themselves deprived by others of their rightful share. Water too was strictly rationed, with only a couple of pints being allowed each day, not just for drinking, but for all other purposes as well.

However, John Bunyan was more favoured than many prisoners, having a family who loved him. Members of the church were also anxious to help him, being deeply grieved that he should be incarcerated in this way. But the first to visit him in prison brought troubling news. His wife, Elizabeth, shocked and dismayed at her husband's imprisonment, had gone into premature labour, and her progress was not encouraging. On the brighter side, Bunyan learnt that his friends were doing their utmost to secure his release. The warrant had stated that Bunyan must remain in jail until the Quarter Sessions the following January unless some local Justice of the Peace could be found willing to arrange bail for him in the meantime.

After Bunyan had been in prison for five or six days, his friends had an idea. The Justice of the Peace at Elstow, a young man who probably remembered John from his Elstow days, might be persuaded to help. Justice Crompton agreed to come to the prison to interview Bunyan and was at first sympathetic. Yes, he might well consider arranging bail terms. Noting Bunyan's noble and upright bearing, he could not imagine that the prisoner would cause any trouble. But later, when he read the warrant, which stated that John's actions had been 'greatly to the disparagement of the government of the Church of England,' he was perplexed. Not since the time of Charles I had there been strictures against laymen, who wished to preach. Independent churches had flourished, and although the status of the national church had now been restored under the new king, no laws had yet been passed prohibiting lay preaching. so had Bunyan been guilty of some other wrongdoing? Why else had he received such a severe indictment? Crompton did not know. Not long appointed as a Justice of the Peace, he became nervous and then refused to be involved in the case.

When the jailer informed Bunyan that this last hope had failed, the prisoner's reaction demonstrated the reality of his trust in God whatever the outcome:

> *I was not at all daunted, but rather glad, and saw evidently*
> *that the Lord had heard me; for before I went down to the*
> *Justice I begged of God that if I might do more good by being at*

liberty than in prison, I might be set at liberty; but if not, his
will be done.

Now he must wait a further seven weeks before his case came to trial but could
add:

I did meet my God sweetly in the prison again, comforting of
me and satisfying of me that it was his will and mind that I
should be there.

SETBACKS

But this setback was not all. Only a day or two later came news that after a pro-
longed labour lasting eight days Elizabeth's baby had at last been born. But frail
and premature, the infant's grasp on life was weak. And soon her baby died. We
can only imagine the effect this incident had upon a man as sensitive as Bunyan,
struggling to accustom himself to the harsh circumstances of prison life. Perhaps
this was one of the lowest points of his early prison experience and it was one
which he recalled with deep sorrow. Writing of these days, he penned some of
the most poignant words in the whole of English literature. In them we have a
glimpse into Bunyan's humanity and need, which still calls out to us across the
centuries from the pages of his record:

I found myself a man, and compassed with infirmities; the
parting with my wife and poor children hath oft been to me in
this place as the pulling the flesh from my bones, and that not
only because I am somewhat too fond of those great mercies, but
also because I should have often brought to my mind the many
hardships, miseries and wants that my poor family was like
to meet with, should I be taken from them, especially my poor
blind child, who lay nearer my heart than all I had besides.

The remembrance of little blind Mary, still only ten years old and much in need
of her father's care, came close to breaking his spirit:

O the thoughts of the hardship I thought my blind one might go under, would break my heart to pieces. Poor child, thought I, what sorrow art thou like to have for thy portion in this world? Thou must be beaten, must beg, suffer hunger, cold, nakedness, and a thousand calamities, though I cannot now endure the wind should blow upon thee. But yet recalling myself, thought I, I must venture you all with God, though it goeth to the quick to leave you. Oh, I saw in this condition I was as a man who was pulling down his house upon the head of his wife and children; yet thought I, I must do it, I must do it.

Yes, he 'must do it', for John Bunyan's conscience and desire to please his God and to preach gave him no alternative. In a long poem entitled *Prison Meditations* written soon after this, Bunyan declares that all he was doing when he was arrested was fulfilling his duty to God:

This was the work I was about
when hands on me were laid,,
'twas this from which they plucked me out
and vilely to me said:
'You heretic, deceiver, come,
to prison you must go;
you preach abroad, and keep not home,
you are the church's foe.'

Seventeenth-century jails did not impose the same restrictions on prisoners as those of today because escape was far less likely. In a community as small as Bedford anyone on the run could easily be tracked down; nor could an escapee get far with poor road conditions and no transport. It also appears that Bunyan's family, and even friends, were fairly free to visit him, bringing food, writing materials and warmer clothes for the winter months. Although Bunyan was too poor to pay for anything apart from bare essentials, his lot was therefore not as dire as that of the friendless and destitute.

A strong tradition exists that John's young blind child Mary used to come to the prison each day with a jug of soup for her father. Probably Elizabeth or another adult accompanied her at first, but the sight of his dearly-loved daughter knocking at the prison gate with his jug of soup must have been the highlight of her father's day. The jug itself is still on display in the Bunyan Museum.

Following Justice Crompton's refusal to arrange bail terms for him, John Bunyan had no alternative but to wait for the next assizes, due to be held early in January. He sincerely hoped that the appointed judges might then be lenient and release him from prison, if only on compassionate grounds. As he thought of Elizabeth's need and of his four children, the youngest only two years old, with nothing to live on but charity, he was consoled by a verse from Scripture: 'Leave thy fatherless children, I will preserve them alive; and let thy widows trust in me' (Jeremiah 49:11). Already John Bunyan was learning to pass a 'sentence of death' on all he held most dear.

CHAPTER 17

THE TRIAL

T he magistrates filed into the Chapel of Herne one by one, taking their seats on the dais with dignity. The Bedford January Quarter Sessions were about to begin. As the tall young prisoner was led in to face his trial, he must have glanced along the imposing line of magistrates. What he saw gave him little cause for hope. Sir John Kelynge of Southill was the senior justice present and chairman of the session. Bunyan knew well that this man had old scores to settle against the Puritan party for he had not forgotten his own eighteen long years of incarceration in Windsor Castle because of his support of the Royalist cause. Bunyan glanced at the four other Justices of the Peace. Not one sympathetic face could he see.

Proceedings began with his indictment against him being read out:

> *John Bunyan of the town of Bedford, labourer, being a person*
> *of such and such conditions, hath devilishly and perniciously*
> *abstained from coming to church to hear Divine service, and is*
> *a common upholder of several unlawful meetings and conventi-*
> *cles, to the great disturbance and distraction of the good subjects*
> *of this kingdom, contrary to the laws of our sovereign Lord the*
> *King.*

If this indictment were not so serious, it would be laughable in view of the circumstances of John's arrest and it was also untrue, for no laws had yet been passed against lay preaching.

'What say you to this?' enquired Sir John Kelynge, eyeing the prisoner before him.

Without hesitation Bunyan replied that he regularly attended the church of God and was in membership with those over whom Christ was Head.

Exasperated, Kelynge clarified the point: 'Do you come to church—you know what I mean, to the parish church?'

'No,' Bunyan answered. 'I do not because I do not find it commanded in the Word of God that I should.' Quickly out of his depth, all Kelynge could reply was: 'But we are commanded to pray.' Soon the other justices chipped in to help him out;. Back and forth went the arguments. Then clearly outmanoeuvred by this common 'labourer', the justices tried insults instead. 'Who is your God—Beelzebub?' demanded one, suggesting that Bunyan was deluded and devil-possessed.. But even this proved ineffectual. Peaceably, the man in the dock ignored such remarks with a secret prayer for God to forgive them.

At last the justices began to address the matter in hand, ordering him 'to leave off his canting', for he had no right to preach. '*Nay, sir,*' protested Bunyan, demonstrating that his call to preach was from God himself and if he left off it would be sinning against his God. Sneers and ribald comments greeted this declaration. Then, seeing he would never convince such prejudiced men, Bunyan made a breathtaking assertion in view of the issues at stake: 'If it is a sin to meet together and seek the face of God, and exhort one another to follow Christ, then I will sin still.'

Twisting his words those five Justices of the Peace jumped on the opportunity to nail their prisoner. 'Then you plead guilty to the indictment, do you not?' said Kelynge, a note of triumph in his voice. The indictment in question was made over sixty years ago under article 35 of the 1593 Elizabethan Conventicle Act—a piece of jurisdiction, long out of date, that Wingate had used to imprison Bunyan.

BACK TO PRISON

Bunyan realized immediately that he was trapped. 'Now, and not till now, I saw I was indicted,' he later wrote. But still he held out. The only 'confession' to which he was prepared to 'plead guilty' was that:

> *...we have many meetings together both to pray to God and to exhort one another, and have the sweet comforting presence of the Lord among us.*

'Of nothing else am I guilty,' he insisted. But it was no use. The justices had chosen to twist Bunyan's words and pronounced their verdict: 'Hear your judgment,' intoned Kelynge:

'You must be had back again to prison, and there lie for three months following; and at three months' end, if you do not submit to go to church to hear Divine service, and leave your preaching, you must be banished (from) the realm. And if (he added menacingly) you be found in this realm without special licence from the king, you must stretch by the neck for it.'

And with that Kelynge ordered the jailer to take Bunyan back to prison.

But it was not Kelynge and his fellow justices who had the final word. Even as the jailer was tugging at his coat sleeve to take him, Bunyan called out, 'If I am out of prison today, I will preach the gospel again tomorrow by the help of God.'

Defiant, courageous and determined, Bunyan returned to prison with a heart thankful to God for his help:

> *I can truly say that my heart was sweetly refreshed in the time of my examination; and also afterwards at my returning to prison.*

Back in prison once more, Bunyan knew he had a further three months in which to consider his position. Only a few days earlier a fellow prisoner, John

Rush, a Quaker from nearby Kempston who had also been imprisoned for his refusal to compromise his conscience, had died after almost a year in prison. 'Perhaps I too will die here', Bunyan must have thought. He had only to agree not to gather a congregation in order to preach and perhaps put in an occasional appearance at the parish church. Then all would be well: he would be restored to Elizabeth and to his young family. But if he even entertained such thoughts, he thrust them from him without delay.

> *Let the rage and malice of men be never so great they can do no more, nor go no farther than God permits them (he reminded himself), but when they have done their worst, 'We know that all things work together for good to them that love God.'*

The prospect of banishment from the country, never again to return to his wife and children except on pain of death, was an alarming one. In days when travel beyond one's immediate community was rare, the thought of 'exile' conjured up wild and fearful mental pictures for Bunyan. Highly imaginative, he could now envisage most dreadful scenarios lying ahead for him.

> *I thought about the sore and sad estate of a banished and exiled condition, how they are exposed to hunger, to cold, to perils, to nakedness, to enemies, and a thousand calamities.*

And, as if all that were not bad enough, perhaps at the end he would 'die in a ditch, like a poor forlorn and desolate sheep.'

But as fast as these morbid prospects invaded his mind, Bunyan manfully banished them by thoughts of the one for whose sake he suffered.

In addition to this, Satan, who had molested John Bunyan so relentlessly in the past, now came back to torment him. And what better way to attack him than to undermine his assurance? If John maintained his stand, he had been crudely told that he would 'stretch by the neck for it'. It was not death itself he feared so much as what lay after death. 'What evidence,' suggested Satan, 'have you for heaven and glory, and an inheritance among them that are sanctified?' In these dark moments of extremity, all Bunyan's confidence drained away. 'Satan laid hard at me and beat me out of heart,' he tells us. And it seemed that God himself had hidden his face from him. 'Perhaps my hopes of heaven are all misplaced after all. I am not fit to die,' thought the distressed prisoner.

This anguish of mind lasted for many weeks. And the end of the three months was drawing ever closer. Again and again he cried out to his God for the comfort and grace he had known formerly, but it seemed the heavens were silent to his need. Then another thought, equally alarming, struck John Bunyan:

> *What would happen if I were taken out to die on the gallows and I should make a scrabbling shift to clamber up the ladder, yet I should either with quaking or other symptoms of faintings, give occasion for the enemy to reproach the way of God and his people?*

He imagined himself on the scaffold with a rope around his neck, ready to be swung into eternity, his knees knocking together with fear. What discredit that would bring on his stand! 'To die with a pale face and tottering knees for such a cause as this' would be grievous indeed.

But an end to Satan's taunting was drawing near. Bunyan recounts it with his customary complete candour:

> *Thus was I tossed for many weeks, and knew not what to do; at last this consideration fell with weight upon me, That it was for the Word and way of God that I was in this condition, wherefore I was engaged not to flinch a hair's breadth from it. I thought also that God might choose whether he would give me comfort now or at the hour of death... I was bound, but he was free; yea it was my duty to stand to his Word.*

With a courage and confidence that had eluded him for many weeks, Bunyan was now able to declare: 'I am for going on and venturing my eternal state with Christ, whether I have comfort here or no.' Then in words as evocative as anything he ever wrote, Bunyan records his decision:

> *If God doth not come in, thought I, I will leap off the ladder*
> *even blindfold into eternity, sink or swim, come heaven or hell,*
> *Lord Jesus, if thou wilt catch me, do; if not, I will venture for*
> *thy name.*

At last Bunyan's troubled mind had found a resting place. With emboldened faith he was able to declare: 'Blessed be God, then, I hope I have an upright heart, for I am resolved, God giving me strength, never to deny my profession, though I have nothing at all for my pains...' So with renewed confidence—even with joy—John Bunyan awaited his forthcoming appearance at the next assizes. But just before it was due, on 3 April 1661, the hearing was postponed.

CHAPTER 18

A COURAGEOUS WOMAN

J ohn Bunyan would have been well aware that the coronation of Charles II
was to take place on 23 April. At any coronation it had become customary
for the new king to declare a general pardon for many of those currently
serving prison sentences—an action to demonstrate his goodwill towards his
subjects. As the prison gates swung open for a considerable number of Bunyan's
fellow prisoners, he discovered to his dismay that his name was conspicuously
absent from every list compiled by the local magistrates

The only answer he could obtain to his repeated enquiries as to why his name
was not included was that he had already been convicted and therefore did not
qualify for the general pardon—a thing that was manifestly untrue, for, as he
stoutly maintained, he had never pleaded guilty to any indictment against him.
One possibility still remained. For a calendar year from the date of the coronation it was possible for those not included in the king's pardon to apply directly
to the king for clemency.

As he pondered the available options, the only expedient John could propose
was that Elizabeth herself should travel to London and present an appeal to the
House of Lords on his behalf. She could speak to William Russell, fifth Earl
of Bedford—one who was known to be sympathetic to Dissenters and other
Nonconformists. And John's brave young wife was prepared to try, though it
must have been a frightening undertaking for a seventeenth-century woman.
The sixty miles or more between Bedford and Westminster would take at least
four days on foot, for it is doubtful whether Elizabeth could afford to travel any

other way. The roads were poor, with highwaymen lying in wait for the unwary, the crowded inns along the way affording little comfort or privacy. But in the early summer of 1661 Elizabeth began her journey, carrying with her John's written petition which explained the circumstances of his request for justice and freedom.

ELIZABETH IN LONDON

Arriving at her destination, this intrepid young woman ventured into the august precincts of the House of Lords, enquiring for the Earl of Bedford. He received her petition sympathetically enough, but said he would need to present it to other members of the House of Lords for a joint decision on the case. This probably spelt the end of Elizabeth's hopes, and sure enough the answer came back that their lordships had no power to release her husband. It is not hard to imagine the crushing disappointment she must have experienced as she prepared to turn homeward, realizing that her endeavours had been fruitless.

Nothing more now remained for John and Elizabeth but to wait for the Midsummer Assizes, due to be held in August. Elizabeth's hopes must have risen when she learnt that Sir Matthew Hale was to be the senior judge on that occasion for he had a reputation for fairness and mercy. Perhaps he could be persuaded to release John. Born in 1609, Hale had held a prominent position in Oliver Cromwell's protectorate government. The Puritan preacher Richard Baxter said of Hale, 'I believe he would have lost all that he had in the world rather than do an unjust act.' Clearly Hale was a fair-minded man but he was also a little nervous on this occasion because he had formerly participated in Cromwell's parliaments and so was anxious not to do anything further to upset the new king.

The other judge at the assizes was to be Judge Thomas Twisden, a man with a reputation for severity, bordering on cruelty. To assist the judges, one or two of the local justices were also present, most noticeably in this case, Sir Henry

Chester of Tilsworth, uncle of Francis Wingate, and one of the original panel of magistrates who had sentenced Bunyan earlier that year.

The grounds of John Bunyan's appeal written on the petition that Elizabeth would present were twofold: firstly, he had been arrested before any new laws against private meetings had been passed, his conviction resting on an obsolete law resurrected for the purpose; and secondly, he had not pleaded guilty to any indictment; the panel of magistrates had only twisted his words and claimed that he had confessed himself guilty.

As the judges alighted from their coach at the door of the Chapel of Herne, where the assizes were to be held, Elizabeth was waiting. As this poor country-woman gazed at these dignitaries in their scarlet robes decorated with ermine, the sight must have been intimidating. Approaching the younger man, whom she knew to be Sir Matthew, Elizabeth presented John's petition. Hale received it 'very mildly', glanced briefly at it and said kindly, 'I will do the best good I can for you and your husband, but,' he added, 'I fear it may be none.'

Slightly heartened by Hale's considerate tone, Elizabeth determined to try again the following day lest Hale had forgotten about her case. With an audacity born of her need, Elizabeth decided on a risky strategy. As the coach carrying the distinguished visitors rumbled down the High Street, Elizabeth stood by the road, with a second copy of John's petition in her hand. As the coach passed she threw the petition in through the open window. Stooping to grab the offensive piece of paper, Judge Twisden, who had clearly been informed of the nature of the case, shouted angrily at Elizabeth that her husband was a convicted man and could not be released unless he would promise not to preach any more.

This was indeed a setback. 'If only,' thought Elizabeth, 'I could speak to Sir Matthew himself, and plead John's cause, I would stand some chance of a hearing.' So on the third day of the assizes, with yet another copy of the petition, this resolute girl pressed through the crowds at the Chapel of Herne and flung herself before Judge Hale as he sat on the bench. Once again Sir Matthew listened sympathetically to Elizabeth's plea, but seeing what was happening, Sir Henry Chester hurried to the bench and spoke to Hale, describing Bunyan as 'a hot-spirited fellow', and assured him that the tinker was indeed lawfully convicted. As one of Sir Matthew's tasks was to check up on the decisions of the local magistrates, it was vital to Chester that nothing amiss should be discovered in their dealings with Bunyan.

Crushed with disappointment, Elizabeth fell back into the crowd as Sir Matthew waived her case aside. All her endeavours had been to no avail. But the High Sheriff, Edmund Wylde, had witnessed the young woman's brave attempt; drawing her aside, he had a further suggestion. If she could speak to Sir Matthew when he was 'off duty', relaxing with the other magistrates and perhaps enjoying a drink together at the nearby Swan Inn, she might stand a better chance. Motivated by her own desperate situation and John's need, Elizabeth summoned up all her courage and, when the hearings were concluded, made her way to the Swan Inn. Pushing her way through the noisy gathering, heart hammering with apprehension, Elizabeth flung herself once more before Judge Hale.

'My lord, I make bold to come once again to your lordship, to know what may be done with my husband,' she faltered.

Astonished and slightly exasperated, Hale replied, 'Woman, I told thee before, I could do thee no good; because they have taken that for a conviction which thy husband spoke at the sessions; and unless something can be done to undo that, I can do thee no good.'

'My lord,' answered Elizabeth, knowing this was her last chance, 'he is kept unlawfully in prison; they clapped him up before there was any proclamation against the meetings; the indictment also is false. Besides, they never asked him whether he was guilty or no; neither did he confess the indictment.'

'My lord, he was lawfully convicted,' shouted some other magistrates standing nearby.

'It is false,' repeated Elizabeth. 'When they said to him, "Do you confess the indictment?" he said only this, that he had been at several meetings, both where there was preaching the Word and prayer, and that they had God's presence among them.'

At this point Judge Twisden joined in, already angry at Elizabeth's persistence. 'What!' he exclaimed, 'Your husband is a breaker of the peace and is convicted by the law.'

Indignation had taken over from fear and Elizabeth's boldness was astonishing as she stood her ground, insisting that the conviction was false. The situation became quite nasty as Justice Chester kept shouting, 'It is recorded. It is recorded,' as if the mere fact that it was recorded made it correct. 'He is a pestilent fellow,' added he, 'there is not such a fellow in the country again'—an unintentional witness to the effect of John Bunyan's preaching.

'What?' intervened Judge Twisden again. 'Will your husband leave preaching? If he will do so, then send for him.'

Elizabeth Bunyan's next comment showed the tenacity and strength of her Christian conviction: 'My lord, he dares not leave preaching as long as he can speak.'

Unable to persuade the judges that John had been falsely convicted, Elizabeth had only her own desperate circumstances left as a plea to move Sir Matthew to compassion. Turning from the angry magistrates, she directed her words solely to him: 'All my husband wants is to follow his calling, that his family might be maintained,' she said, adding with a degree of pathos which obviously touched Sir Matthew, 'My lord, I have four small children that cannot help themselves, of which one is blind, and have nothing to live upon but the charity of good people.'

Four small children—how could so young a woman, probably little more than nineteen or twenty, have such a family? Hale wondered.

'My lord, I am but mother-in-law (i.e. stepmother) to them, having not been married to him yet two full years. Indeed, I was with child when my husband was first apprehended; but being young and unaccustomed to such things, I being dismayed at the news, fell into labour, and so continued for eight days, and then was delivered, but my child died.'

'Alas, poor woman,' said Hale with genuine sympathy. But seeing that his fellow judge was being swayed in favour of this persistent woman, Twisden intervened. 'She makes poverty her cloak,' he said with a sneer. 'Her husband is better maintained by running up and down a-preaching than by following his calling.'

'What is his calling?' enquired Hale.

'A tinker, my lord, a tinker,' cried a chorus of voices.

Elizabeth was quick on the rebound. 'Yes, and because he is a tinker and a poor man, therefore he is despised and cannot have justice.'

Clearly Hale was now taking Elizabeth seriously, but still felt there was little he could do in the circumstances. He now spoke 'very mildly' to her: 'I tell thee, woman, seeing it is so, that they have taken what thy husband spake for a conviction, thou must either apply thyself to the king, or sue out his pardon or get a writ of error.' This last alternative upset Justice Chester all the more. A 'writ of error' would obviously reflect badly on the court decision which he had helped to make. 'My lord,' he said vehemently, 'he will preach and do what he lists (i.e. likes).'

'He preaches nothing but the Word of God,' retorted Elizabeth promptly.

'He, preach the Word of God!' snarled Judge Twisden, lunging towards Elizabeth as though he would dearly like to strike her across the face. 'He runneth up and down and doth harm.'

'No, my lord,' interrupted Elizabeth, 'it is not so; God hath owned him and done much good by him.'

'God!' responded Twisden angrily. 'His doctrine is the doctrine of the devil.'

With all the verve of a woman who knew she had right on her side, Elizabeth responded, directing her words straight to Judge Twisden: 'My lord, when the righteous Judge shall appear, it will be known that his doctrine is not the doctrine of the devil.'

Understanding full well that Elizabeth was implying that he was an *unrighteous* judge, Twisden could only comment to Hale, 'My Lord, 'do not mind her, but send her away.'

Caught in the crossfire of this exchange, Hale was in a difficult position. He could not be seen to dissent publicly from his fellow judge. All he could do was to apologize to Elizabeth and repeat his former advice, but he emphasized once again that her best and cheapest option was to get a writ of error. At this point Justice Chester appeared even angrier, and although Elizabeth begged again and again that John should be sent for out of prison to plead his own case, she could soon see that nothing more could be done.

Bursting into tears, Elizabeth pushed her way out of the crowded Swan Inn. But, as she afterwards explained to John when she told him all that had transpired, these were not tears of self-pity, nor even of grief at the failure of her endeavours, but 'to think of the sad account such poor creatures will have to give at the coming of the Lord, when they shall there answer for all things whatsoever they have done in the body whether it be good or whether it be bad'.

Clearly Elizabeth was a worthy wife of such a man as John Bunyan.

CHAPTER 19

LIVING ON THE INVISIBLE GOD

F ollowing the midsummer assizes, the next session when the cases of Bedford prisoners were to be heard was due in November 1661. Once more Bunyan made strenuous efforts to gain a hearing before the judiciary of the day. He fully expected that on this occasion his indictment would come up for review, but the assizes came and went, and his name was again omitted from any list presented to the magistrates. Nothing remained but for him to face another cold winter in Bedford Jail.

All Bunyan's hopes of release in the near future faded. He thought of his young family in their need, of Elizabeth, of the believers whom he loved and had served, of his young converts in the faith for whom he could now do little. Certainly he was called upon to 'pass a sentence of death' upon all that he had held dear, and instead 'to live upon God that is invisible'. Like Moses, who also 'endured as seeing him who is invisible', so too John Bunyan found great 'reward' through his sufferings. 'I never had in all my life so great an inlet into the word of God as now,' he declared, adding:

> *Those Scriptures that I saw nothing in before are made in this place and state to shine upon me. Jesus Christ also was never more real and apparent than now; here I have seen him and felt him indeed.*

But it was far from easy. Satan took every opportunity to taunt the prisoner; sometimes fears troubled him and those wild imaginations that he had known in his youth returned to harass and distress him. But at such times he found the tender grace of God to be his support and comfort. Sometimes his comforts were so overwhelming that he confesses that 'Were it lawful, I could pray for greater trouble, for the greater comfort's sake.' Turning his thoughts into verse, John Bunyan wrote:

> *For though men keep my outward man*
> *within their locks and bars,*
> *yet by the faith of Christ I can*
> *mount higher than the stars.*
> *Their fetters cannot spirits tame,*
> *nor tie up God from me;*
> *my faith and hope they cannot lame,*
> *above them I shall be.*

WRITING IN CHAINS

Meanwhile the situation for Dissenters, such as the Baptists and Independents, was looking increasingly gloomy. On 19 April 1662 the Bill of Uniformity requiring any who held any church office to 'declare consent to all and everything contained in the revised *Book of Common Prayer*' became law and 24 August—a day that would be known as Black St Bartholomew's Day—was the deadline set by the government. Over two thousand preachers and schoolmasters felt unable to consent with a clear conscience and were forthwith ejected from their livings, their homes and their incomes. Bunyan would have known that many of his associates and friends were suffering severely. On that day the sufferings which Bunyan had been enduring for almost two years became the lot of many.

Burning with indignation against such compulsory use of the *Book of Common Prayer* and the suffering it had brought to those who refused to use all or part of it, John Bunyan took up his pen once more and began to write a treatise on the character of real prayer. Magistrates might silence the voice of the preacher by incarcerating him in a cold prison, but they had not reckoned on the power of his pen. And before long Bunyan would produce a remarkable book bearing the title, *A Discourse Touching Prayer*. This was Bunyan's first prison book and is a spiritual gem, reprinted many times and still in print.

A stained-glass window in the Bunyan Meeting Free Church inserted in 1978 depicts a well-dressed man with a seraphic smile on his face, hair neatly combed, sitting by a window, quill in hand and blank paper before him. With a sturdy table on which to write, the sun streaming in through the window onto the coloured floor tiles, this window presents an idealistic but thoroughly erroneous picture of John Bunyan's prison conditions. How he managed to write at all amidst those overcrowded, filthy, rat-infested surroundings, with the groans of prisoners resounding in his ears and the ever-present clank of chains reminding him of the death sentence imposed on many inmates, is astonishing.

Yet write he did, perhaps with his paper resting on his knee, his quills and ink faithfully brought to the prison by Elizabeth, or even by his blind child Mary, now twelve years of age. Gradually, as the weeks lengthened into months, Bunyan began to realize that any hopes of his own release were far distant. What will happen to Elizabeth and the children, he must have asked himself a hundred times? But at least he could do his best to provide for them. Being a practical man, Bunyan quickly mastered the skill of fitting metal tags on the ends of the long laces used to secure boots and shoes. One who spent some time in prison with Bunyan records that he made 'many hundred gross' of such tags for sale. Possibly he stood at the prison gate himself trying to attract the attention of passers-by, or his child Mary may have sold them in the marketplace, her blindness and need touching the sympathy and purses of those bustling around. Added to this, Bunyan wrote a number of shorter poems and articles, probably for sale to support the family. Every spare moment found the prisoner busy either writing, reading or twisting and fastening tags

Opportunities for private prayer in the dirty, degrading and crowded prison must have been non-existent. And yet in spirit John Bunyan soared above his surroundings as he communed with God, receiving new strength for his circumstances. But still the weary prison days stretched out before him. He may have heard various items of news concerning events taking place outside his prison and he would be encouraged to know that the Bedford Independent Church was continuing to meet as they were able, although always in different homes and locations.

To know that many young believers to whom he himself had preached were receiving pastoral care and were remaining faithful despite the difficulties and persecutions which were now their lot, would have brought Bunyan much consolation. And at least he could instruct them by his writings, and this he did in a book he called *Christian Behaviour*, written in his third year in prison. Still anticipating that at any moment the jailer could unlock the gate and summon him forth to the scaffold, he concludes this work by saying: 'Thus have I in few words written to you before I die...because I desire that you may have the life laid up for all them that believe in the Lord Jesus and love one another when I am deceased...'

Nothing remains to mark the spot where this 'prisoner of hope' suffered, prayed and wrote apart from a plaque in the pavement indicating where the old prison once stood but these written memorials still have power to move the heart more effectively than any other monument.

CHAPTER 20

AMID THE DARKNESS

The sweet sound of someone playing a flute could be heard coming from the upper prison day room in Bedford County Jail. Who could be creating such music in the midst of the squalor and degradation of a prison? None other than John Bunyan, prisoner of the Crown, a man who would rather obey his God than buy his freedom at the expense of his conscience. But when the jailer came up to investigate the source of the music, he was puzzled to find nothing more than his prisoner occupied as usual, perhaps making metal tags.

From his youth Bunyan had enjoyed music and had once made himself a small violin carefully crafted from metal and inscribed with his name. Whether he had been able to bring his violin into the prison with him, we do not know. But one day he had an idea. If he removed one leg from his stool, hollowed it out and notched it in the correct places, he could make an acceptable flute. Then if he heard the jailer approaching, he had only to slip the stool leg quickly back into place. This explained the mystery of the music the jailer had heard.

INCREASING PRESSURES

The situation for the persecuted Dissenters was becoming steadily more oppressive. Whereas the pastors and teachers had suffered under the terms of the 1662 Act of Uniformity, now it was the turn of the people. In May 1664 the first Conventicle Act was passed. This legislation ordered that no more than five people in addition to the immediate members of a family should gather together for any form of religious activity. The rank and file of Baptists, Independents, Presbyterians, Quakers, and any other grouping outside the Established Church, now became the target of this new Act. From the government's point of view this was seen as a way of stamping out not only religious dissent, but any secret gathering that might be plotting an uprising of some kind.

The new Conventicle Act was harsh in its terms. For anyone discovered at a service of worship, however innocent it might be, a fine of £5, or three months imprisonment, was immediately imposed. For a second offence the penalty was doubled. A third offence called for a fine of £100, or seven years banishment. Private homes could be suddenly surrounded and searched to count the number of people gathered together. On occasions a small group of friends gathered together at a funeral could face the same penalties if more than five were present.

Often men and women were too poor to pay such exorbitant fines; then the consequences could be still worse. Armed with a warrant to seize whatever goods they could find in lieu of payment, constables would ransack the homes of the poor, sometimes even in the middle of the night. Kitchen implements, bedding, tools vital for trade and even food for sick children were all taken at will, often condemning the victim to abject poverty. Rarely would sufferers put up any resistance — indeed there was little they could do in their own defence. A number of congregations devised their own means of escape. As magistrates could only administer justice within the borders of their respective counties, Dissenters might worship in meeting houses which bordered several counties. If a look-out man warned of the approach of magistrates from one county, the congregation could quickly disappear into another to be beyond their reach. Even so, the prisons were now packed to overflowing with men and women who had been discovered worshipping in some hidden corner.

PREACHING IN PRISON

Although it was little compensation to John Bunyan that his fellow Christians were also suffering, he now had an unexpected bonus of sweet companionship within those prison walls. Sometimes a whole congregation caught worshipping was marched straight to prison. If he must be severed from his congregation, John Bunyan now discovered that a congregation had come to him. We can only imagine the depth of joy and fellowship those suffering Christians experienced as they worshipped their God together in such circumstances, well knowing that no cruel constable could burst in and molest them further.

A number of John Bunyan's most memorable printed sermons started out as messages addressed to his fellow prisoners. One remarkable example is found in a work entitled *The Holy City or The New Jerusalem*. Rising to preach amid the squalid surroundings of the jail, John Bunyan directed the gaze of his hearers beyond those strong walls that held them captive, beyond 'the lumber and cumber of this world' to the beauties of the New Jerusalem—a city of gold, the true church of Jesus Christ.

In this graphic sermon, which Bunyan later expanded into a lengthy treatise, he began to reveal his genius for allegory. Imprisoned as he was within a gloomy jail where the brightness of full daylight rarely penetrated, one of the most lovely features of the heavenly city for Bunyan was its light. The very thought of a day when all darkness will be dispelled forever brought him joy. In a rare reference to his own circumstances, he writes wistfully, 'You know how especially pleasant (this light) is to such men that have for several years been held in the chains of affliction.'

John Bunyan is almost lost for words as he describes this eternal state:

> *Then will be a golden world... It will be then always summer, always sunshine, always pleasant, green, beautiful, fruitful and beautiful to the sons of God ... the mountains shall drop down new wine, and the hills shall flow with milk... O blessedness!*

THE GREAT PLAGUE

But all was far from beautiful in the world outside those prison wall. Only the previous year Holland had been ravaged by plague. And by early spring 1665 it was clear that the dreaded scourge was spreading among the crowded London streets. The summer months of 1665 were exceptionally hot, and by mid-July the death toll had soared to more than 1,000 a week. In August it had reached over 6,000 dead in a single week and by September had peaked at 7,265. Daniel Defoe, in his account of these frightening days, reports that 40,000 dogs and 200,000 cats were killed, as it was feared that these domestic animals might be carrying the disease. In fact this was the worst possible action to take, for the real culprits were the fleas carried by the black rats. In the absence of their natural predators, these rats multiplied and the plague spread.

Terrified by the rapid increase and the virulence of the disease, the Lord Mayor ordered that all victims and their families should be locked into their homes together. The houses were to be marked with a red cross and sealed up for forty days until either all were dead, or the disease had been conquered. Guards posted outside the houses refused to respond to the desperate cries from within, and families were known to break down the walls of their homes in order to escape. Nurses and those appointed to care for the sick were forced to carry coloured sticks so that the public could give them a wide berth. And each evening the death carts trundled down the roads with the doleful cry: 'Bring out your dead.' Eventually the plague would kill one in five of all Londoners.

Records of the devastation caused by the Black Death in previous epidemics sent a chill of fear throughout the land. During the fourteenth-century outbreak whole villages had been wiped out in a matter of days. Rumours of the fearful death rate in London would have reached John Bunyan in prison. Doubtless some of his friends in the city had already died. Perhaps the plague would soon spread beyond the capital, eventually sweeping through the country. Many who observed these things were convinced that this outbreak of the plague was evidence of the righteous anger of God on the nation because of the cruel measures inflicted on many innocent Dissenters.

The County Jail in Bedford would be particularly vulnerable to the infection due to its filth and overcrowding. But, rather than brood on the very real possibility of the contagion reaping its grim harvest in the prison and among his own family and friends, John Bunyan busied himself with further writing. It may even have been the possibility of imminent death that caused him to begin an account of his own early life and conversion, especially for the sake of his converts, and perhaps also for his children and Elizabeth.

However, as we have already seen, *Grace Abounding to the Chief of Sinners* was not intended primarily as autobiography. Bunyan carefully explains in his preface that he was addressing his words to his own spiritual children, those converted through his preaching, in order to point out a way of deliverance from the temptations and the pain of spiritual anguish which he had suffered.

It would appear that Bunyan wrote the bulk of *Grace Abounding* during 1665 and had it ready for the printer either late in that year or early in 1666. But who would print it? Perhaps someone had recommended a young publisher named George Larkin, and it was to him that the prisoner entrusted the first edition of this remarkable book. Until 1883, a period of almost two hundred years, it was thought that no copies of this first edition had survived. Then a single copy came to light. A probable reason for the disappearance of all other copies of the first edition was the devastating Great Fire of London of 1666 that consumed vast stockpiles of books stored in London warehouses. But *Grace Abounding to the Chief of Sinners* remains among the most outstanding spiritual autobiographies of all time.

CHAPTER 21

A MASTERPIECE IN THE MAKING

Whenen Thomas Farynor, Charles II's baker, forgot to shut down his oven fire one night in September 1666, he could not know that his carelessness would ignite the greatest conflagration that London had ever known. Sparks from his fire fell on an adjacent pile of kindling wood, and by the time Farynor had been in bed for three hours his shop and house were ablaze. A high wind carried the sparks from the burning shop in Pudding Lane to the Star Inn in nearby Fish Street Hill. Soon the hay provided to feed the animals of travellers staying the night at the inn caught fire… and so the fire spread.

THE GREAT FIRE AND A SHORT FREEDOM

In a city of buildings largely half-timbered and covered with pitch, many with thatched roofs, the risk of fire was high. For five dreadful days the inferno consumed everything in its path. By order of the king many homes were purposely blown up by gunpowder to check the course of the blaze. Before the fire was finally brought under control, one and a half square miles of the city had been reduced to cinders. Eighty-seven of London's old churches had succumbed to the flames and more than 13,000 homes had been destroyed. To many it seemed that the Great Fire, following so soon after the Great Plague, was God's response to the Conventicle Act—this new cruel measure instigated by the Cavalier Parliament in order to crush any dissent from the national church.

Because the plague was still affecting different parts of the country extra precautions were clearly needed in Bedford. This probably explains why John Bunyan was released from prison for a few short months at this time. The grime and rat infestation of the prison made it a vulnerable target, and prison staff may well have been depleted as a result of either sickness or fear. Plague did indeed find some forty victims from an area of the town not far from the jail. To have her husband home at last must have been a deep joy for Elizabeth. Her courage and faithfulness over the years, mothering John's family and supporting John himself, make this woman's name shine out in the annals of Christian heroism. John's blind elder daughter, Mary, now sixteen, was far from well; his second daughter, also named Elizabeth, was twelve and the boys, John and Thomas, were ten and eight. Before long John's second wife had the added happiness of knowing that she was expecting her own child, a compensation for the baby she had lost when John was first arrested.

But John Bunyan's freedom did not last long. And we can well imagine that the prison floor seemed harder and the straw filthier when he found himself back in his old surroundings. John must have found this second imprisonment hard indeed. During his first six years in prison he had written and published at least nine treatises, sermons or poems. Now he temporarily fell silent, publishing nothing between the years 1666 and 1672, although, as we shall see, he was still engaged in writing. It is also likely that his blind daughter Mary, whom he had described as 'nearer my heart than all I had besides', died at about this time. Perhaps more than ever before, with Elizabeth expecting another child, John found that he must 'pass a sentence of death' on all he held most dear. Yet, as he had written earlier, such afflictions made him 'look to God through Christ to help me and carry me through this world'.

These events might well have caused him to recall a sermon he had once preached on 1 Corinthians 9:24: 'So run that ye may obtain.' Very probably this sermon, which he had entitled *The Heavenly Footman*, was actually preached before he was first imprisoned in 1660, but faced with his present grievous circumstances, John Bunyan might well have realized the relevance of this message with its call for endurance in the heavenly race. 'THEY THAT WILL HAVE HEAVEN MUST RUN FOR IT', he wrote in capitals on his paper as he began to urge the vital importance of active perseverance in the Christian race. Perhaps he preached the sermon again to his fellow prisoners, for some might be tempted to succumb to despair under their trials.

THE BIRTH OF 'PILGRIM'S PROGRESS'

The Heavenly Footman, subtitled *A Description of the Man that Gets to Heaven,* is perhaps one of the most convicting and searching books that Bunyan ever wrote. He allows no one to remain complacent. 'Everyone that runneth doth not obtain the prize,' he cautions, and adds, '... there be many that do run, yea, and run far too, who yet miss of the crown at the end of the race.'

However, the date when Bunyan was writing up this powerful sermon is highly significant for another reason — a reason which he himself explains:

> *And thus it was: I writing of the Way*
> *and race of saints in this our gospel day*
> *fell suddenly into an allegory*
> *about their journey and the Way to Glory;*
> *in more than twenty things, which I set down;*
> *this done, I twenty more had in my crown,*
> *and they again began to multiply*
> *Like sparks that from the coals do fly...*

So it was that while he was urging men and women to run for heaven regardless of hindrances that Bunyan first conceived the idea for his great allegory, *The Pilgrim's Progress.* The exact words from *The Heavenly Footman* which grabbed his imagination and sent new ideas tumbling through his brain might well have been these:

> *Because the way is long (I speak metaphorically), and there is many a dirty step, many a high hill, much work to do, a wicked heart, world and devil to overcome... Thou must run a long*

and tedious journey through the vast howling wilderness, before thou come to the land of promise.

And so, laying aside his present manuscript for the time being and reaching for a fresh wad of paper, Bunyan began to scribble down the new ideas that were flooding his mind. Addressing them as if they were living people, he writes:

Nay then, thought I, if that you breed so fast
I'll put you by yourselves, lest you at last
should prove ad infinitum and eat out
the book that I already am about.

Taking Bunyan's own testimony that the seed thoughts for *The Pilgrim's Progress* sprang from a book he was already writing on the 'race of saints in this our gospel day', we may safely assume that this book was indeed *The Heavenly Footman*. He must therefore have started to write his great allegory in about 1667–68. When the ideas first came to him, John Bunyan had no thought of turning them into a book; it was merely as a diversion from his present depressing circumstances. *The Heavenly Footman* and *The Pilgrim's Progress* must therefore be regarded as complementing each other, both urging his readers to persevere in the race for heaven.

Although *The Pilgrim's Progress* takes the crown of all Bunyan's writings, *The Heavenly Footman* has had a profound effect on many Christians both in the past and in our own day, and to read it cannot fail to spur the believer onwards in his race to heaven.

CHAPTER 22

FROM A DEN IN THE WILDERNESS

'**A**s I walked through the wilderness of this world, I lighted on a certain place where was a den.' These are among the best-known words in all literature. With them John Bunyan introduces his readers to what he modestly calls 'my scribble' in his versified 'Apology' for *The Pilgrim's Progress*. Setting the tone for his entire book, he immediately unites two opposite concepts. In his autobiography, *Grace Abounding*, Bunyan had described his prison as a 'Lion's Den', and now, in case his readers need reminding, his new book also has its genesis in such a den—the harsh circumstances of a seventeenth-century prison, where Dissenters like Bunyan languished, many spending the best years of their adult lives there.

Together with this earthy and material concept of a 'den'—a small confined space—Bunyan uses the image of a wilderness, conveying the sense of a wide and trackless place. This alerts us to the fact that *The Pilgrim's Progress* is not only born out of the grim realism of the prison, but is also an allegory. The author is creating a backdrop for a right understanding of all that follows. The 'wilderness' concept clearly springs directly from the Scriptures for God describes himself as the One who led his people 'through that great and terrible wilderness, wherein were fiery serpents, and scorpions, and drought...' (Deuteronomy 8:15). The narrative of a dream was a natural medium for Bunyan to begin to express the thoughts that were crowding into his mind for he had been ever a dreamer.

Most of Bunyan's first readers would immediately relate this unfolding story to his autobiography, *Grace Abounding to the Chief of Sinners*. His own anguish under the burden of his sins is clearly in John Bunyan's mind as he sits in his 'den' penning these memorable words. The Slough of Despond, which Bedford people will readily point out to visitors as they view the marshy land near John's childhood home of Elstow, also has its equivalent sense in Bunyan's own experience as he struggles toward the gate to which Evangelist has pointed.

Nor can we be surprised when we discover that the next crisis facing the aspiring Pilgrim before he reaches the Wicket Gate is the temptation to think that a careful observation of the demands of the law of God will be an adequate means of obtaining God's favour and his salvation. The subsequent failure of such an attempt had all but crushed John Bunyan's own spirit. Bowed low beneath the burden on his back, Pilgrim now meets up with Worldly Wiseman, who, plausibly enough, directs him to the home of Legality by way of Mount Sinai where, he assures him, his burden will quickly be removed. But, following Worldly Wiseman's directions, the troubled man soon finds his burden heavier still and is overcome by fear:

> *There came flashes of fire out of the Hill that made Christian*
> *afraid that he should be burned: here therefore he sweat and*
> *did quake for fear.*

This is a vivid pictorial representation of the teaching Bunyan had set out almost ten years earlier in *The Doctrine of Law and Grace Unfolded*. The influence of Martin Luther at a crucial time in Bunyan's life and the liberating effect he had known in reading Luther's *Commentary on the Epistle to the Galatians* is clearly evident in this part of his dream. As he trembles under the overhanging mountainside of Sinai, Christian is rescued by Evangelist, severely admonished and set back on the right path towards the Wicket Gate. Before long he is knocking importunately at the gate, and Goodwill, a representation of Christ himself, as Bunyan later makes clear, pulls the bedraggled seeker to the safety within.

A wicket gate, as the *Oxford English Dictionary* points out, is a narrow door, often set within a larger one, and corresponds here to the 'strait gate' of the Lord's teaching. Again tradition indicates a small door in the parish church in Elstow as a possible origin for Bunyan's imagery. Whether this was so or not, we cannot be certain, as he does not tell us himself, but certainly this Wicket Gate symbolizes far more in *The Pilgrim's Progress* than a mere gate. As Goodwill, the keeper of the gate, is a representation of Christ, so the gate itself captures the same image, for Christ declares himself to be both the door and the way to heaven.

John Bunyan undoubtedly uses entry through the Wicket Gate as a symbol of spiritual conversion. It is to the gate that Evangelist directs the troubled man, and once through the gate Goodwill assures the pilgrim that 'An open door is set before thee and no man can shut it.' The gate stands at the head of the way, and as Christian journeys he meets a number of phoney travellers who have not entered by the gate, but had jumped over a wall or chosen some other entry. None of these are seen to be genuine pilgrims. With quickened interest the reader turns the pages of *The Pilgrim's Progress* to discover how the pilgrim loses his burden; and we may well imagine that, absorbed in his dream-story, Bunyan also found his own prison circumstances easier to bear.

Far from the scenes of degradation and hopelessness within Bedford jail, important political changes were taking place which would eventually ease the pressure on men and women of faith like John Bunyan. The Great Plague, followed so soon by the Great Fire, had troubled and unsettled the people. Many felt certain that the face of God was turned in anger towards the land, the prime cause undoubtedly being the persecution of godly men and women.

Absolute power under the King rested on the Lord Chancellor, Edward Hyde, Earl of Clarendon, an intolerant and merciless man. But now this man became the scapegoat for the general sense of discontent and unjust laws. He fell from power, fleeing to France. In his place, five Privy Councillors took over the effective government of the country, becoming known as the Cabal, an acronym made up of the initial letters of their names. These formed a more tolerant regime and even though Bunyan was still busy chronicling the progress of his pilgrim, he would have been well aware of the easing of pressure in the country.

Adding to this new spirit of hopefulness came the safe birth of Elizabeth's child, Sarah— conceived during John's short release in 1666. The recent death of his blind daughter Mary had been a deep grief to John, making the birth of another daughter a source of much-needed comfort. At last, after seven years of caring for her stepchildren, Elizabeth had a child of her own to nurture and love. And for John himself, the possibility that he might soon be released from prison to preach freely and to support his young family once more was a great consolation.

Meanwhile the ideas for Christian's pilgrimage to the Celestial City were still pouring into Bunyan's mind. Before his pilgrim could lose his burden at the Place of Deliverance - the cross, Goodwill had directed him to the House of the Interpreter, where he would learn valuable lessons to help him on his journey: the vital importance of perseverance and of striving ceaselessly to attain that crown of gold at the end of the journey. This too had been the subject of *The Heavenly Footman*, and is the dominant theme of the entire book John was now writing. The Interpreter gave the new pilgrim many other instructions before he set out on his journey once more.

Then we reach a critical moment: 'Now I saw in my dream… the Cross. There it was, standing by the wayside on a small elevation. Not far away the pilgrim saw what appeared to be a large hole. As he approached the Cross he felt the cords binding the burden to his back snapping one by one. Suddenly it fell off and began to roll down the hillside until it came to the hole, or 'sepulchure' where it fell in. Then Christian exclaims joyfully, 'And I saw it no more'.

Christian's reaction to these things is one of unutterable joy as he weeps with sheer relief and happiness. Then three 'Shining Ones' appear, giving him pledges of this new-found assurance. One declares, 'Thy sins be forgiven thee'; a second strips off his rags, clothing him with 'a change of raiment' or a 'broidered coat', as he later describes it; while the third sets a distinguishing mark on his forehead and gives him a sealed scroll, which he must read often and guard carefully, for, like a passport, it would be a guarantee of his welcome in the Celestial City.

Giving 'three leaps for joy,' Christian proceeds on his way, singing:

> *Thus far did I come laden with my sin;*
> *nor could aught ease the grief that I was in*
> *till I came hither; What a place is this! ...*
> *Blest Cross! blest Sepulchre! Blest rather be*
> *The man that there was put to shame for me!*

Many have noticed the similarities between John Bunyan's autobiography, *Grace Abounding to the Chief of Sinners,* and *The Pilgrim's Progress.* Long hours spent meditating on the nature of the Christian life had given the prisoner in Bedford jail an abundance of material for 'this my scribble' as he described it—for new ideas crowded into his mind, so quickly, that he scarcely had time to write them down.

But after eight years in prison, and now at the age of forty, John Bunyan must have wondered at times whether he would end his days within those stern walls, incarcerated by the state for conscience' sake. At one point, as he wrote the allegory of his *pilgrim's journey through this alien world* he imagines Christian and his companion pilgrim, Hopeful, as poor captives of Giant Despair in Doubting Castle. We may well surmise that Bunyan's story became almost autobiographical at this point and particularly when Christian plumbed the depths even contemplating Giant Despair's suggestion that he should take his own life.

> *Brother, said Christian* (to his fellow prisoner)*, what shall we do? The life that we now live is miserable! For my part I know not whether 'tis best to live thus, or to die out of hand ... the grave is more easy for me than this dungeon.*

Only Hopeful's words, warning of the sin of suicide and exhorting him to patience and hope, raise the pilgrim's thoughts above such despondency. Then, after finding new strength through prayer, Christian suddenly remembers that he carries in his pocket a key called Promise which can open any lock in Doubting Castle. With this he and Hopeful escape from the grasp of Giant Despair.

Another aspect of Bunyan's genius as he develops his allegory lies in his choice of names for his various characters. These are people we may all know well, and with Bunyan we either smile gently at the caricature, or else take to heart the warning of the dangers that such individuals pose. Some of these personify those whom Bunyan knew before his conversion: Legality and his son Civility, and of course Mr Worldly Wiseman, all dubious types who mislead pilgrims. Obstinate and Pliable epitomize many who show initial interest in the Christian faith and then draw back. Talkative, the son of Say-well, is full of religious conversation but has little or no understanding of inward heart-religion.

Christian will meet many perplexities along the way, but Bunyan's ethic of trial and affliction for his pilgrims is a positive one. Even when Faithful, another fellow traveller, is cruelly put to death by the angry mob in Vanity Fair, Bunyan refuses to detail his sufferings but tells us rather:

Now I saw that there stood behind the multitude a chariot
and a couple of horses waiting for Faithful, who was taken up
into it and straightway was carried up through the clouds with
sound of trumpet, the nearest way to the Celestial Gate.

RENEWED PERSECUTION

We are not surprised to learn that at about the time that Bunyan was writing these things, his well-loved fellow Christians in the Bedford meeting were being plunged into a period of intense suffering. Since the fall of Edward Hyde, the Lord Chancellor, and the establishment of the five ministers of state known as the Cabal, the situation for Dissenters had eased considerably. Heartened by this, many began to meet openly again. New meeting houses were built, and pastors who had been banished were emboldened to appear in their former pulpits. But all this increased activity on the part of these churches soon provoked a negative reaction against them. Parliament became alarmed and yet more anxious to suppress conventicles, fearing that they were hotbeds of revolution.

Then on 11 April 1670 came an offensive against Dissenters more vicious than anything they had known in recent years. The Second Conventicle Act was passed by Parliament. It hit out at the Dissenting churches with added ferocity coupled with brutal reprisals against anyone discovered worshipping except at a parish church. Just one month later, on 15 May 1670, the Bedford Meeting felt the full impact of the heavy hand of the law. Doors were broken down, homes ransacked and personal belongings 'distrained', or seized in lieu of money, if these worshippers were unable to pay the hefty fines. Secret informers intent on rewards could be spying night and day to report anyone found at such gatherings.

There is a fifteen-page account of the sufferings of the Bedford church, now held in the British Library that gives many examples of the barbaric cruelty Bunyan's fellow believers endured. Among many examples we read of a widow, a Mrs Mary Tilney, who was caught at a service of worship. Her home was emptied: tables, chairs, cupboards, mattresses, blankets all seized, even down to the sheets on her bed. Her neighbours wept openly at this manifest robbery—a thing which grieved the kindly woman more than her own losses. In another instance a weaver called Thomas Thorowgood, from the nearby village of Cotton End, dared to allow his home to be used for a meeting. Betrayed by the careless chatter of a little child, the premises were raided and Thorowgood, who could not pay the £20 fine, was dispossessed of all he had, right down to the loom with which he earned his living. Despite the fact that fines were to be doubled if these people were caught worshipping again at an illegal conventicle, the Bedford Meeting church members did not hesitate to gather the next Sunday.

It is not hard to imagine the distress which John Bunyan must have experienced as a helpless prisoner unable to share or relieve the sufferings of his fellow church members. But for him there remained nothing he could do but take up his pen again and continue his dream, little realising that one day his words would be of strong consolation to future generations of God's people. In these final, well-loved chapters of *The Pilgrim's Progress* men and women the world over have reaped untold benefit from the sufferings of this one member of the Independent church at Bedford.

CHAPTER 23

A STRANGE CONCLUSION
AND A NEW FUTURE

A
s John Bunyan sat in his sordid prison cell, with little natural light penetrating the gloom, his thoughts were far away. In his mind's eye he could see two men standing in a land of extraordinary beauty:

Here they heard continually the singing of birds and saw every day the flowers appear in the earth... In this country the sun shineth night and day, wherefore this was beyond the Valley of the Shadow of Death and also out of reach of Giant Despair, neither could they from this place so much as see Doubting Castle. Here they were within sight of the city they were going to.

Christian and Hopeful had arrived in Beulah Land—a country that in Bunyan's mind lay in immediate sight of the Celestial City. Only the River of Death— that deep and bridgeless river—remained to be crossed before the travellers reached the Celestial City, their ultimate destination. Bunyan was under no illusions about the nature of death. In the margin of his story he wrote, 'Death is not welcome to Nature, though by it we pass from this world into glory.' He had experienced the anguish of bereavement early in life when both his mother and sister died within a single month. In addition his first wife and his well-loved blind daughter Mary had been taken from him in death.

So in Bunyan's allegory Christian finds the waters dark and menacing when he enters that last river. He fears he will be lost. Crying out, 'I sink in deep waters, the billows go over my head,' he sees all his sins of a lifetime rising up against him to condemn him. Satan can often launch his most bitter assaults at a dying believer, and in *The Pilgrim's Progress* Bunyan describes Christian's 'horror of Mind and Heart—fears that he should die in that river and never obtain Entrance in at the Gate'. Hopeful, true to his name, finds the passage easier, and struggles to keep Christian's head above the waters. 'Brother, I see the Gate and Men standing by to receive us,' he calls out to encourage his struggling companion.

At last Christian cries in a loud voice, 'Oh, I see him again! And he tells me, "When thou passest through the Waters I will be with thee..."' Finally he feels solid ground under his feet once more. 'Then they both took courage and the enemy was after that as still as a stone, until they were gone over.' Together the two pilgrims reach the farther bank, and Bunyan's description of the glories of heaven awaiting them on the farther shore is among the finest in all literature:

> *Now I saw in my dream that these two men went in at the Gate, and lo, as they entered, they were transfigured: and they had raiment put on that shone like Gold... Then I heard in my dream that all the bells in the City rang again for joy... Now just as the gates were opened to let in the men, I looked in after them; and behold the City shone like the sun, the streets also were paved with gold...*

Little wonder, then, that John Bunyan, sitting in his unwelcome prison, was carried away by his own account and could add sadly, '... and after that they shut up the gates: which when I had seen, I wished myself among them.' We can almost imagine him looking around his gloomy 'den', with the glory still shining in his eyes, and wishing that he too could be there.

And so the narrative ends—but not quite. *The Pilgrim's Progress* was never intended to be a mere story, full of entertainment value for his readers. Like all Bunyan's best works, it was evangelistic before anything else. Although he had been prevented from preaching to the crowds who once thronged to hear him, this book is effectively a sermon from start to finish. Again and again he warns his readers of the dangers of entering the pilgrim path in any other way but by the Wicket Gate. A number of characters in *The Pilgrim's Progress* appear to begin well, but fall at various hurdles along the way. Their fate is to be taken as a warning to all would-be pilgrims that the way to heaven is both narrow and hard and pilgrims must persevere to the end.

Bunyan's strange concluding paragraph to *The Pilgrim's Progress* should be read in that light and then comes as no surprise. In his dream he sees Ignorance, that 'brisk lad' with whom Christian and Hopeful had already held long and fruitless conversations, approaching the river. Although they had tried to persuade him again and again that his own righteousness could never be enough to gain entrance to the Celestial City, he would not listen. Instead he insisted that his own heart was sufficiently good and pure. Ignorance then crosses the river easily with the help of a ferryman named Vain Hope, but when he reaches the gate of the City he is unable to produce a certificate to prove himself one of the King's true subjects. Bound hand and foot, Ignorance is taken to a door in the side of the hill and thrust in. Bunyan ends his book with these sombre words: 'Then I saw that there was a Way to Hell even from the Gates of Heaven as well as from the City of Destruction.'

Certainly, from a literary perspective, such an ending 'spoils' Bunyan's book, but, as we noted, his purpose is primarily evangelistic. Why, then, does he single out Ignorance for such a dreadful end? He had entered the pilgrim path through 'a crooked lane' rather than the Wicket Gate, but many other so-called pilgrims had also deviated from the right path in different ways. The answer perhaps lies in the fact that Ignorance persistently denied a doctrine that Bunyan held to be of supreme importance: the doctrine of the righteousness of Christ credited to the believer as a free gift. Martin Luther's *Commentary on Galatians* had emphasized this teaching, bringing enormous release to Bunyan at the beginning of his spiritual life. It had been 'gold in my trunk' to discover that:

> *… it was not my good frame of heart that made my righteous-*
> *ness better, nor yet my bad frame that made my righteousness*
> *worse; for my righteousness was Jesus Christ himself, the same*
> *yesterday and today, and forever.*

By this incident Bunyan is teaching us that to reject the righteousness provided by Christ to make us acceptable in the sight of God, is a sin that leads to ever-lasting loss and banishment from the presence of God.

THE HOPE OF FREEDOM

As John Bunyan was putting the finishing touches to his great allegory import-ant changes were afoot on the national scene which would profoundly affect Bunyan's future. Charles II hid his cunning and devious nature under a play-boy exterior; for, although he appeared outwardly little interested in anything apart from women, sport and spaniels, he was in fact plotting major changes for the country. First, he schemed to dispense with Parliament and rule alone as his father had done; next he planned to bring his country back to the Roman Catholic fold. Already a covert Catholic himself he was preparing to remodel the English church, subservient to Rome in all but the papacy.

But there was a problem. To do this Charles would need to extend religious tol-eration to English Catholics who now faced the same penal laws as the Dissent-ers and Nonconformists. The only course open to him lay in granting religious freedom to all outside the Established Church. In that way he hoped that his real motive to reinstate Catholicism might pass undetected. So, calling on his royal prerogative, the king announced a Declaration of Religious Indulgence on 15 March 1672.

Up and down the country prison doors swung open, with hundreds leaving their foul and dingy cells as free men and women. But there were conditions as well. To prevent religious anarchy, the king stipulated that, upon application, he was willing to grant licences to as many places of worship as might be required for Dissenting gatherings and also to give licences to certain named preachers who would be permitted to officiate at services of worship.

CALLED TO MINISTER

Three months before this date, anticipating that the king would soon announce such a declaration, the church in Bedford made a significant decision—one that would affect John Bunyan for the rest of his life. In October 1671 the proposal to appoint him to be pastor of the church had been discussed at a church gathering. Since then the church members had given themselves to 'much seeking God by prayer and sober conference.' And on 21 December 1671, at a full church meeting held no doubt in some secret location, those gathered made their solemn resolution: John Bunyan was to be officially appointed to undertake the pastoral oversight of the church as soon as he was released.

Buffeted over many years by the storms of persecution, Bunyan had stood unbowed and firm. When he was first imprisoned, as a zealous young man recently turned thirty-two, he had displayed outstanding gifts of preaching and leadership. Tall, auburn-haired and vigorous with clear fresh features, he was youthful, eager and dedicated in the service of God. Now at forty-four years of age, matured by suffering and experience, John Bunyan was a much older-looking man, but in every way even more equipped to lead a church which had itself been tried in the storm.

Although he was already allowed a measure of freedom, in view of the king's Declaration of Indulgence, John's release was not granted automatically. He must still apply to have his name included in the lists of those eligible for discharge on the grounds that his sole 'misdemeanour' had been to worship or preach at a conventicle. Many prisoners might otherwise attempt to escape from jail under false pretences.

At last the Bedfordshire County Sheriff confirmed that Bunyan's release was legitimate, and that attending conventicles had indeed been his only offence. Even then, not until 13 September 1672 was his pardon officially ratified by the King's Great Seal and he was able to pack up his few belongings for good. Perhaps tucked under one arm he carried a sheaf of papers containing 'this my scribble'—a story of a lonely man who had set out on pilgrimage to the Celestial City and of all the trials he had encountered before reaching his goal. What to do with the manuscript, he hardly knew. But for the time being he had enough matters of concern on his mind to delay any decision on the matter.

A portrait is extant dated 1673—the year after John Bunyan emerged from prison—showing a very different-looking man from the more popular pencil sketch by Robert White. The face looks pale and a little strained—a contrast with the surviving description of him as a man with a fresh-looking, reddish complexion. Maybe this was the result of long years of living in semi-darkened surroundings. But the eyes are intense and piercing—eyes that had looked on the filth and degradation of a seventeenth-century jail, yet eyes that had looked into the Celestial City and seen its glories.

HOME AT LAST

But the joy of John Bunyan's homecoming was not without its shadows. In many respects he was a stranger to his own children, for Elizabeth had brought up his family single-handedly for almost twelve years. When John was first thrust into prison on that November day in 1660, his older son was only four. Now he was a young man of sixteen, probably as tall as his father. Thomas, who had been just two years old, was now fourteen. Possibly Thomas resented the deprivations suffered by the family, and had allowed his father's imprisonment to rankle and embitter his spirit. Certainly he had missed his father's strong hand of discipline on his life and may already have been a difficult young person to handle. Not many years after this we discover Thomas involved in petty crime, much to the shame and embarrassment of his godly father and stepmother. Blind Mary had died, and John's second daughter Elizabeth was now a young woman of eighteen; his young daughter, Sarah, child of his second marriage, was an energetic five-year-old.

Nor were things straightforward on the business front. His son John had been training as a metal worker, doubtless with the hope of one day taking over his father's brazier business. But the business itself was in ruins; as one contemporary records, '… his temporal affairs were gone to wreck, and he had as to them to begin again as he had newly come into the world.' All his former customers had found other tradesmen to undertake their work, and if the ex-prisoner wished to start up again he would need to establish new contacts—no easy thing at his age.

But in spite of his problems, Bunyan rejoiced to be out of that dank and fetid prison at last. Turning his back on Bedford County Jail that September day in 1672, he would have walked along Mill Street before reaching his home in St Cuthbert's Street where Elizabeth and the family awaited him. As he passed by, however, his eyes would have turned naturally to an old orchard that lay a little below street level to his right. Nearby stood an equally old barn, the real object of Bunyan's interest. It could easily be turned into a meeting place for the church, at least as a temporary measure. Since being turned out of St John's in June 1660, the church had known no settled home. Often they would gather in small groups in secret, and they would always be moving from place to place for fear of informers. At present the orchard and barn both belonged to Justice Crompton, the very one who had refused to arrange bail for Bunyan when he was first imprisoned in 1660. But with the sum of £50 offered for the barn, Crompton was tempted to agree to the sale.

It is not hard to imagine the flurry of activity as church members speedily began to strip down the old building, perhaps apply a coat or two of whitewash and furnish it with benches, ready for the day when their new pastor would preach the opening services. A fresh opportunity of service had begun for Christ's suffering servant, and before long John and his wife Elizabeth were cheered by the birth of another child, their last, Joseph.

With fresh opportunities and joys now opening up before him, John Bunyan was glad to put the pain of those last twelve years behind him and give all his energies in service to his God and to his Bedford congregation while he had the opportunity.

CHAPTER 24

THE BEDFORD PASTOR

Although the Dissenters celebrated their new-found liberties in 1672, no right-minded person supposed that days of persecution were gone forever. Their freedom could only be tenuous at best, and if a fickle king or antagonistic Parliament were to reverse the present policies, further days of harassment could well lie ahead.

At the same time a war that had been declared against Holland in March 1672 was not going well for England, particularly when Spain and Austria joined the fray to support the Dutch. In desperation Charles II recalled his Parliament in order to provide more finance for this expensive war. Parliament was willing enough to oblige, but at a price—Charles must repeal the Declaration of Indulgence. A growing fear of the King's hidden intentions to reinstate Catholicism was clearly behind this condition. So when Parliament was recalled in March 1673, it promptly repealed the Declaration with a humiliated king being forced to break open the royal seal on the Declaration with his own hands.

All liberties granted to Dissenters were withdrawn once more and added to this the Cabal ministry collapsed as Sir Thomas Osborne, Earl of Danby, came to power. A rabid opponent of any deviation from the Church of England, whether Dissenting or Catholic, Sir Thomas was intent on introducing yet harsher measures to deal with those who wished to worship outside the orbit of the Established Church in an attempt to crush the spirit of Nonconformity totally.

But this proved impossible. A year or more of freedom had led to an explosion of Dissenting causes: new buildings had been licensed, their preachers issued with the King's own permission to officiate. No preacher seemed quite sure, however, whether the repeal of the Declaration of Indulgence also meant that his licence to preach had been cancelled. In the absence of any overruling directive to the contrary, most were determined to continue their ministries. And the government knew that unless such licences could be officially annulled, there was little they could do to curb the influence of men like John Bunyan and his fellow preachers. Nevertheless, the church in Bedford was deeply concerned about the situation, with the minute book recording days of prayer and humiliation to seek God's favour and intervention.

Meanwhile, regardless of the darkening situation and while opportunities remained, John Bunyan gave himself steadfastly and unremittingly to his work as a preacher and pastor. Not only did he preach penetrating and powerful sermons aimed at disturbing the conscience, he put them into print. To preach such sermons was bound to arouse fresh opposition. For twelve years his antagonists had tried and failed to silence the voice of the preacher. But now his opponents tried an even more potent method to bring John Bunyan's reputation to ruins—scandal. In 1674 John Bunyan faced one of the supreme trials of his life—one that led him to defend himself hotly and indignantly in print.

FRESH PERSECUTION

First, the rumours were spread about that he 'was a witch, a Jesuit, a highwayman and the like'. So ridiculous were such accusations that Bunyan could dismiss them with little more than a metaphorical wave of the hand and the comment, 'God knows that I am innocent', adding that he would pray that his accusers might be brought to repentance.

But when the rumour-mongers suggested that he 'had my misses, my whores, my bastards, yea two wives at once', Bunyan was incensed, but also recognized that Christ had forewarned his followers that men would say 'all manner of evil against you falsely for my sake.' Accusations came to a head early in 1674, when Bunyan had been pastor for little more than two years.

The charge concerned a young woman named Agnes Beaumont. On 31 October 1672 the name 'Agniss Behement' was entered on the church register—the first entry in John's own handwriting. Agnes, an articulate and intelligent young woman, was a twenty-two-year-old farmer's daughter. She has left a detailed account of the events which occurred on a bitterly cold February day in 1674—events which sparked off a malicious character assassination of John Bunyan.

Agnes kept house for her widowed father, a man who had shown passing spiritual concern, but had then become a virulent opponent of Bunyan and the Bedford Meeting. All Agnes wanted was to be at the meetings and to hear Bunyan preach, a thing her father was now reluctant to permit. Then came a day when the Lord's Supper was to be celebrated at Gamlingay, seven miles from her home. For a whole week Agnes had been praying that God would soften her father's heart so that he would allow her to attend.

At last the young woman gained the coveted permission but, as her brother and his wife were also going, and using the only available horse, Agnes would need a lift to Gamlingay, She asked a fellow church member, John Wilson, to call at the farm to take her riding pillion on his horse. Such an arrangement was not considered at all improper; indeed, it was a regular practice in those days. Great was the girl's disappointment as she waited patiently by the farm gate for Wilson to come and eventually realized that her plans had gone wrong and that he was not coming. But she brushed away her tears when she heard another horse and rider approaching the farm—and who should it be but John Bunyan himself, on his own way to the meeting?

Too shy to ask for a lift, Agnes appealed to her brother to ask Bunyan on her behalf. Knowing the antagonism of the girl's father, Bunyan refused, despite the earnest pleas. Also he was well aware that his enemies were just waiting for some supposed indiscretion on his part. Only after seeing Agnes's distress and hearing her repeated entreaties, along with a promise that she would accept the consequences, whatever they might be, did Bunyan at last agree to take her. But they were spotted—first by Agnes's father, who threatened to pull her off the horse if he could catch them, and then by the local Church of England curate who caught sight of them as they rode along, He looked gleefully at them. John Bunyan had given his enemies the very opportunity for which they had been waiting.

The consequences for Agnes were serious. Not only did her father lock her out of the house for the following two nights, but when he died unexpectedly three days later of a heart attack, she was accused of poisoning him. The case was brought to trial; had she been found guilty, she would undoubtedly have faced the death penalty. But who had helped Agnes plan the supposed murder? Who had supplied the poison? The gossips had a ready answer. Why, surely, it must have been John Bunyan, they whispered. Agnes's story, told in her own artless style and with breathless intensity, has been printed many times under the title *Behind Mr Bunyan,* complete with dramatic line drawings depicting events as they unfolded.

But if the situation was serious for Agnes, who was eventually pronounced innocent, it was yet more so for Bunyan. Adding eleven indignant paragraphs to be included in the next edition of *Grace Abounding,* he struggled to clear his name:

> *My foes have missed their mark in this their shooting at me. I am not the man. I wish that they themselves be guiltless. If all the fornicators and adulterers in England were hanged by the neck till they be dead, John Bunyan, the object of their envy, would be still alive and well.*

John Bunyan realized that his real enemy was none other than the Evil One himself, and the plan behind these 'reproaches and slanders to make me vile among my countrymen' was in order that 'if possible my preaching might be made of none effect.'

Without doubt these unseemly accusations against Bunyan succeeded to some small degree otherwise he would not have felt that he must defend himself as robustly as he did; but there is no evidence that this incident caused any permanent damage to his reputation. In the wisdom of God, Bunyan declared, he had always been 'shy of women from my … conversion until now.' So circumspect had he been in all such relationships that he had constantly avoided being alone with women members of his church—maintaining a standard of integrity higher than was the general practice. Few therefore could take such libellous charges against the new pastor seriously.

CHAPTER 25

TENUOUS LIBERTY

J ohn Bunyan was on the run. It was February 1675. Parliament, composed of many who were virulently opposed to any toleration of dissent from the Church of England, had won the day and compelled the king to issue a proclamation declaring that even the licences granted to Dissenting preachers were retracted. Anyone caught officiating at a religious service other than in accordance with the state church liturgy would henceforth be liable for a fine of £20 for a first offence and £40 for any subsequent offence— a charge well above the average wage for a year. If the preacher were unable to pay, his household goods could be commandeered up to the worth of his fine. The only mitigating clause stipulated that nothing could be taken from his home unless the 'offender' himself was present.

So to protect Elizabeth and the children, and also his church, Bunyan had no option other than to go into hiding. It must have been a wrench to leave his family once more. Joseph, his youngest son, was little more than two at the time and Sarah barely eight. As magistrates had jurisdiction only over their own counties, it was vital for John to leave Bedfordshire. But where could he go? The most likely answer is that he did not stay long in any one place to avoid causing trouble for his hosts.

A number of locations in the counties around Bedford have strong associations with John Bunyan. Some of these links may well have been created at this time of extremity. Many Independent and Baptist meeting places had secret escape routes so that if the local constables were seen approaching, the preacher could 'disappear' before they arrived. One 'pulpit' which Bunyan is reputed to have used could also double up as a high-backed pew, so hiding the preacher from sight if necessary. This pulpit can still be seen today, stored in the vestry at Breachwood Green Baptist Church, near Hitchin.

Some cottages could provide a concealed cupboard or even an unused chimney into which a hunted preacher could squeeze until the danger was past. An old chimney stack in Coleman Green, near Wheathampstead, is all that remains of a cottage where Bunyan is reputed to have stayed when preaching nearby. It now bears an inscription to that effect, while the public house on the green opposite, taking advantage of the association, is called *The John Bunyan*.

Perhaps the most evocative of all the places associated with Bunyan's name is Wainwood Dell, not far from Hitchin. Anyone who ventures into the woods can still discover among the trees what appears to be a large circular hollow shaped like a natural 'amphitheatre' that is now overgrown and wild. To this spot, so tradition tells us, John Bunyan's congregation would creep at dead of night and listen with rapt attention to their preacher as he sought to raise their eyes above the struggles and sufferings of this life to see the glory in store for the people of God.

In all likelihood much of Bunyan's time was actually spent in the relative safety of London, for it would be harder to track him down in the city. Another purpose he had in visiting London was to seek advice from his friends as to whether to allow his 'scribble'—that story he had written of a pilgrim travelling to the Celestial City—to be printed or not. To many good men such a novel form of writing came as something of a shock. Not all were happy about it. As Bunyan tells us in his versified 'Apology':

> *Well, when I thus had put my ends together,*
> *I show'd them others, that I might see whether*
> *they would condemn them, or them justify:*
> *and some said, Let them live; some, let them die.*

Some said, John, print it; others said, Not so.
Some said, It might do good, others said, No.
Now was I in a strait, and did not see
which was the best thing to be done by me.

Torn by all the conflicting opinions, John made up his own mind:

At last I thought, Since ye are thus divided,
I print it will; and so the case decided.

BACK TO BEDFORD—AND PRISON

After eighteen months of effective homelessness John Bunyan made another critical decision. He would return to Bedford. Elizabeth needed him; the children were being deprived of their father; the church had no pastor. But what would happen if he were arrested and imprisoned again? Perhaps John felt it was a risk he must take. And so as 1676 drew to a close he returned. But the joy of his homecoming was soon muted. With his old enemy William Foster on the prowl to ensure that Bunyan was brought to account, the outcome was predictable. A loud rap on the door and a sharp demand for 'John Bunyan' was all too soon followed by the familiar walk 'home' to prison once more.

And so John Bunyan was back behind bars. His family and church must have felt unimaginable dismay as the well-loved preacher's liberty was forfeited once more after only four years of relative freedom. Tradition has always maintained that during this second imprisonment John was put into the Town Clink, situated on the picturesque old bridge that once spanned the River Ouse. The present-day bridge now bears a plaque alerting visitors to the fact that the town's renowned former resident was once locked in the old Clink.

Some have questioned, however, whether this was indeed Bunyan's prison, suggesting that in all probability he would have been sent back to the County Jail. But John Brown, Bunyan's most important early biographer, vigorously asserts that the Clink on the bridge was indeed the scene of Bunyan's second imprisonment. Brown, himself the pastor of the Bedford Meeting from 1864 to 1903, rests his contention on a strong unbroken tradition backed up by other church members and notably by Bunyan's own great-granddaughter. Another possible pointer to the Town Clink on the bridge being Bunyan's prison was the incidental discovery of a ring marked 'JB' buried in the rubble when the prison was finally demolished in 1765.

Snatched from his valued work of preaching and watching over the spiritual lives of his church members, the imprisoned pastor would naturally have turned his mind to his writing. Doubtless he had brought with him that manuscript written during his earlier imprisonment which he had called *The Pilgrim's Progress*. While some could see little good in his work and advised him against publishing it, others were encouraging him to go ahead. The only way to discover who was right, Bunyan had decided, was to test out the market.

Although Bunyan filled as much time a possible with his writing, it must have been difficult to keep a sense of despair at bay in the circumstances. Days turned to weeks, and weeks to months, and still there seemed no prospect of his release. Perhaps he was going to die in that damp, desolate place for he was now almost fifty years of age, and his health had already been undermined by his previous long imprisonment.

JOHN OWEN AND FREEDOM

But God had not forgotten the sufferings of his faithful servant. Though poor and forgotten by those in authority, John Bunyan had influential friends, and none more so than Dr John Owen. A prominent Puritan theologian, and pastor of Leadenhall Street Congregational Church in London, Owen was one who actually had the ear of the king himself. Occasionally Owen had asked Bunyan to fill his own pulpit.

'Why do you listen to a tinker prate?' Charles II had disdainfully asked Owen.

'Had I the tinker's abilities (to preach), please your Majesty,' replied Owen, 'I would most gladly relinquish my learning.' And now John Owen grieved for the treatment meted out to Bunyan. When a mutual friend spoke to him on his behalf, Owen decided to act. His opinion carried some weight with the Bishop of Lincoln, Thomas Barlow, into whose diocese Bedford fell. Barlow had been Owen's tutor during his student days at Oxford, and was therefore well disposed towards him. Writing to Barlow, Owen pleaded Bunyan's cause. Barlow hesitated, anxious for his own reputation and eventually suggested that Owen approach the Chancellor, Lord Finch, first; if he agreed, then Barlow would be happy to oblige and endorse the conditions for Bunyan's release. Only after the Chancellor had given his approval did Barlow at last consent to ratify the decision and the prison doors swung open for John Bunyan.

A free man once more, John Bunyan's priority in the summer of 1677 was to find a publisher for *The Pilgrim's Progress*. Fears of a fresh wave of persecution against Dissenters were abroad, and Bunyan knew he must act without delay. Dr John Owen had used a certain Nathaniel Ponder to publish his own writing, and it may well be that he recommended him to Bunyan. Ponder had already risked much to publish the work of Independent preachers, and was prepared to take on Bunyan's new and intriguing 'scribble'. In December 1677, the book was submitted to the Stationers' Hall for a licence; this was granted the following February, and before long the first copies of this unusual book were coming off the press at *The Peacock in the Poultrey*, in Cornhill, London.

So popular did the first edition of *The Pilgrim's Progress* prove to be that it sold out within months, and still the public was clamouring for more. Just one highly valued copy of this first edition remains today; it is kept in a padded box in the British Library, with viewing only allowed under close supervision. This slim volume, containing 233 pages and sold for one shilling and six pence, is in beautiful condition, after having been discovered virtually unused in some nobleman's library.

Astonished by the success of his publishing venture, Bunyan immediately began to work on a new and improved second edition. A number of passages were inserted, including some among the better-known portions of the entire book. Perhaps most important is the passage that includes Christian's encounter with Mr Worldly Wiseman. This vivid extract contains the disingenuous advice given by Worldly Wiseman to Christian, sending him to the village of Morality to get rid of his burden. It continues with the terrified pilgrim cowering under Mount Sinai, fearing that the rocks will fall on his head, until Evangelist meets him again, reproves him and directs him back to the Wicket Gate. A number of other small changes are also to be found in this second edition, including a paragraph in which Bunyan parodies the residents of a town called Fair-Speech, introducing us to such characters as Lord Turnabout, Mr Smooth-man, Mr Anything, and the parson, Mr Two-Tongues—undoubtedly Bunyan had met a number of such people during his long imprisonments.

Hard days still lay ahead for Dissenters, and John Bunyan knew that at any moment he might find himself trapped into a situation in which he could be thrown back into prison. But for the moment this deeply tried Christian must have experienced much joy as he noted in amazement the overwhelming popularity of *The Pilgrim's Progress*.

CHAPTER 26

PREACHER AND WRITER

Released from prison once more, John Bunyan must have sensed that his time was short. In fact he had little more than ten years of life left and these he packed with an unsparing schedule of preaching and writing—a schedule which would have baffled many strong men who had not suffered any of the dreadful conditions that Bunyan had known. The political situation was tenuous, with plots and counter plots sending waves of fear though the population. Nobody felt safe. The fear of Catholicism rose to a new pitch because Charles II's brother James, heir to the throne, was a fanatical Catholic. His abhorrence of Dissenters spelt disaster for any worshipping according to conscience. Cries of 'No Popery' rang out across the streets of London, while effigies of the pope were burnt each November to mark the anniversary of the accession of Elizabeth I. But strangely it was the Dissenters such as members of the Bedford Meeting that suffered most.

Fines, more ruinous than anything imposed before, were levied against those caught in the act of worship. Goods were confiscated, leaving families with no means of support. Once more the prisons were packed with Dissenters who were either unable or unwilling to pay these exorbitant fines. Not all Dissenters stood quietly by while their property and livelihoods were destroyed; the records of the Broadmead Baptist Church in Bristol give a number of instances of intense resistance to such downright robbery conducted in the name of the law.

Understandably, churches once more went 'underground', meeting in woods at dead of night, in dells, barns, or any secret place hidden from the prying eyes of informers. After December 1681 we have only a few intermittent records of the Bedford Meeting, and virtually none at all between 1683 and 1688. Clearly Bunyan's church too went into hiding and certainly feared to record any of its activities. Caring for the spiritual life of the church under such conditions cannot have been easy. Troubles seemed to press in on every hand. Bunyan could well say with the apostle Paul that he had been 'in perils of my own countrymen... in perils in the city... in perils among false brethren... besides... that which comes upon me daily, the care of all the churches.'

Although deeply troubled about the situation, Bunyan never allowed himself an idle moment. His publisher, Nathaniel Ponder, who had now acquired the nickname 'Bunyan Ponder', was busy producing a third edition of *The Pilgrim's Progress*. Little more than a year had elapsed since the first had been published, and still the public were clamouring for more.

Much of Bunyan's time during 1679, however, was taken up with a far different project. As a follow-up to *The Pilgrim's Progress*, he had planned to write the story of a life journey that led in the opposite direction from the Celestial City—the story of one who travelled through this world on a downward path leading to hell. The idea had been simmering in his mind for some time and the result was a book with the grim title, *The Life and Death of Mr Badman*.

In creating the misdemeanours of this fictitious character, Bunyan packs into his story many of his own observations of the vices to which unregenerate men can stoop. Much of his material may well have been gleaned from his twelve years in Bedford Jail, as he came into contact with villains guilty of gross acts of wickedness. However, in view of the state of the nation, it may well be that Bunyan was also looking beyond the wicked life of one individual and had a message for a nation that had deliberately turned away from the high ideals of Puritan godliness and was condoning a licentious lifestyle practised both by the court of Charles II and by the ordinary citizen.

This follow-up book to *The Pilgrim's Progress* was printed by Nathaniel Ponder in 1680, but in view of its subject, we are not surprised that it did not enjoy the same reception as its predecessor—a fact that may have set John Bunyan thinking about the possibility of some other sequel to his highly popular book.

TIMES OF TRIAL

If times were hard in England, conditions were even worse for the Covenanters in Scotland. Most wanted nothing more than to worship their God peaceably according to the dictates of conscience, and like the Dissenters, refusing to compromise with the strictures of the state church. But the 1680s, known as the Killing Times, were days when men, women and young people were hounded, hunted and slaughtered without mercy. Stories like that of the two Margarets, Margaret Wilson and Margaret MacLachlan—the former a girl of eighteen and the latter aged sixty-three—tied to posts and drowned by the incoming tide in the Solway Firth for refusing to 'conform', are familiar. So too are many other accounts of appalling injustice and cruelty. Whether John Bunyan knew of these fearsome acts of wickedness, we do not know.

During these years Bunyan himself was tireless in his toils, both in preaching and writing. Exposed to all weather conditions, he could be found wherever he might secretly and safely gather a congregation. It is not hard to imagine the difficulties of such a ministry. The state of the roads was appalling; some of them merely rutted tracks with deep potholes that turned to muddy ponds in winter, or wet weather. Gingerly picking its way along, Bunyan's horse carried him, often at dead of night, to many isolated places where eager congregations were expecting him. The nickname 'Bishop Bunyan', playfully given to one whose dislike of episcopacy was a byword, relates to these days, as such a ministry took him not only to the villages of Bedfordshire, but to all the surrounding counties, and further afield. Before the intense persecution made it impossible, Bunyan could also be found preaching in London from time to time.

By 1682 eight editions of *The Pilgrim's Progress* had come off Nathaniel Ponder's presses, though scarcely four years had passed since its first publication—a fact that added enormously to Ponder's personal success as a printer. And still the public clamoured for more from Bunyan's pen. Probably the very fact of his popularity proved a safeguard from a further prison sentence at this time.

THE HOLY WAR

Against this background of unrest, fear and the unrestrained progress of evil, John Bunyan at last wrote his second great allegory, a complicated story which he entitled *The Holy War*. This marathon work ran to some 102,000 words and was written in little more than ten months—an astonishing achievement with a quill for a pen and nothing else beside paper.

Bunyan takes as his theme the vicious and endless battle between Emmanuel, representing Christ, and Diabolus, portraying the devil that rages over the town of Mansoul. Completed early in 1682, *The Holy War* was printed by Newman and Alsop. It may be that the popularity of *The Pilgrim's Progress* gave Nathaniel Ponder little time for work on anything else. Demand for the first allegory was still as great as ever. Some even refused to believe that an unlettered tinker who had spent more than twelve years in a degrading prison could possibly be the author of such a work of genius. In a versified 'advertisement' attached to *The Holy War*, Bunyan was ready with his reply, delivered with a measure of indignation.

> *Some say The Pilgrim's Progress is not mine,*
> *insinuating as if I would shine*
> *in name and fame by the worth of another,*
> *like some made rich by robbing of their brother…*
> *I scorn it: John such dirt-heap never was*
> *since God converted him.*

As in the opening lines of *The Pilgrim's Progress*, so in *The Holy War*, Bunyan introduces his readers to his subject with a personal allusion regarding its origins. The words are simple and memorable:

> *In my travels, as I walked through many regions and countries,*

> *it was my chance to happen into that famous continent of Universe; a very large and spacious country it is....*

And among the diverse towns and areas 'in this gallant country of Universe,' Bunyan comes across 'a fair and delicate town, a corporation, called Mansoul.' So beautiful was this town in its original state that he reports that 'There is not its equal under the whole heaven.' This stately town of Mansoul was the possession of King Shaddai, and in it he had built for himself a pleasing palace. Peace reigned in Mansoul: 'There was not a rascal, rogue or traitorous person then within the walls.' Depicting man as first created by God, Bunyan presents a splendid word-picture of life before the Fall. Then onto the scene comes Diabolus, 'a great and mighty prince, and yet both poor and beggarly', who, with his fallen angels, seeks to conquer and possess the town of Mansoul as vengeance upon King Shaddai for casting him out of heaven. And he succeeds.

In his introductory poem Bunyan aligns himself personally with Mansoul, both in its original glory and in its subsequent shame:

> *For my part, I (myself) was in the town,*
> *both when 'twas set up, and when pulling down.*
> *I saw Diabolus in his possession,*
> *and Mansoul also under his oppression.*

He knew only too well from his godless youth what it meant to be 'pulled down' as he served Diabolus, or the devil.

Mansoul had five gates, each representing one of the senses, but it is through Ear gate and Eye gate that Diabolus and his host of fallen angels seek to make their most subtle attack. Because the town cannot be taken without the consent of its people, Diabolus seeks by smooth words to persuade them to open the gates, suggesting, as he did to Eve in the Garden of Eden, that King Shaddai was depriving the town of its rightful benefits. Captain Resistance, who guarded Ear gate, is shot dead; Captain Innocency also dies, and Diabolus, with his evil troops, enters the town and proceeds to take up residence in Heart Castle. The town is remodelled; Shaddai's laws are revoked and his image, which stood in the marketplace, defaced.

So when King Shaddai learns of the tragic fall of Mansoul into the grip of Diabolus, he sends four brave captains, accompanied by an army of 40,000, to lead an assault to regain the town. These captains, Boanerges, Conviction, Judgment and Execution, represent the initial blasts made against the soul because of the broken law of God—an experience which Bunyan himself knew all too well.

These captains fail to recapture the town until at last Emmanuel himself raises an army and conquers Mansoul. But the story does not end there. We learn of Diabolus's repeated attempts to retake the town. Despite times when it seems he has succeeded, Emmanuel wins back his Mansoul. Depicted in lines both simple and splendid, the character of Prince Emmanuel dominates the whole, both when he is present, visiting and cherishing his people, and when absent, grieving at their backsliding. Among some of the most striking and evocative words which Bunyan ever wrote are found in Emmanuel's last charge to Mansoul. Gathering the whole town into the marketplace, he addresses them in unforgettable language:

> You, my Mansoul, and the beloved of my heart, many and great are the privileges I have bestowed upon you. I have singled you out from others and have chosen you to myself, not for your worthiness, but for my own sake.

To restore them from their backsliding he tells them :

> It was I who made thy sweet bitter, thy day night, thy smooth ways thorny, O Mansoul, that thou mightest find me, and in thy finding, find thine own health, happiness and salvation.

And the future for Mansoul will be glorious as Bunyan describes in words of outstanding beauty, the joys that await them in Emmanuel's own land. *The Holy*

War may be more difficult to read than *The Pilgrim's Progress*, but it more than repays the effort.

Few author's are without their critics, however, and John Bunyan received his share even though he has been coupled with John Milton as the two greatest writers of the seventeenth century England. Some writers even published their own 'Pilgrim' stories to correct what they deemed to be Bunyan's theological errors, while others added the initials 'JB' to their work to gain a quick readership. At last Bunyan felt compelled to write his own sequel to *The Pilgrim's Progress* and in 1684 published his Part 2. Again in the form of a dream he tells how Christiana, Bunyan's wife, her four boys and her friend Mercy set out for the Celestial City. The journey follows much the same pattern and has passages of intensity and beauty, though never as favoured as Part 1.

None, however, would deny the pathos and depth of the final chapter as Christiana and her friends cross the Last River one by one. In all likelihood, John Bunyan was conscious that his own strength was failing and was meditating often on the nature of death and the glory beyond. The prison years followed by incessant preaching and writing—for he was the author of fifty-nine separate books had aged him beyond his years. Most significant is Bunyan's account of a pilgrim named Mr Standfast. As he crosses the river he speaks to those waiting on the bank:

> *I see myself now at the end of my journey, my toilsome days are ended. I am going now to see that head that was crowned with thorns, and that face that was spit upon for me. I have formerly lived by hearsay and faith; but now I go where I shall live by sight, and shall be with him in whose company I delight myself. I have loved to hear my Lord spoken of; and wherever I have seen the print of his shoe in the earth, there I have coveted to set my foot too... His voice to me has been most sweet; and his countenance I have more desired than they that have most desired the light of the sun... Now while he was thus in dis-*

course, his countenance changed, his strong man bowed under him; and after he had said, 'Take me, for I come unto thee,' he ceased to be seen of them.

It is impossible to read such words without thinking of John Bunyan himself, one to whom the name Standfast most aptly applies.

CHAPTER 27

CROSSING THE RIVER

I t was mid-August 1688, and although John Bunyan had been ill recently he was anxious to fulful a preaching engagement in London, a journey that would take him two days in his weakened condition. Riding steadily west over roads that were often little more than rough tracks, he broke his journey over night with friends in Reading. Next morning he turned his horse's head towards London but as he did so no doubt glanced anxiously at the darkening sky and hoped that the threatened storm would not break before he reached his destination.

The atmosphere grew ever more sultry and humid. Clearly the storm was now imminent. Anxiously spurring his horse onwards, Bunyan knew he must reach Snow Hill in Holborn by nightfall where John Strudwick had invited him to stay during his visit to London. Strudwick, who ran a grocery business known as *The Sign of the Star* from his home, had become a valued friend in recent years.

Before long John caught the sound of the first ominous rumblings of thunder: then flashes of lightning tore through the sky and finally torrential rain began to sheet down. With little protection against the elements, both horse and rider were soon drenched. The roads, never much better than rubble-filled ditches, turned to mud tracks and then to running streams. Had Bunyan sought shelter along the way, perhaps in Maidenhead or Slough, all might have been well, but he struggled on, blinding rain driving into his eyes. At last he reached the outskirts of London. Heading north, he finally arrived in Snow Hill, shivering and exhausted, and was knocking thankfully at the door of John Strudwick's tall four-story home.

Alarmed at his state, Strudwick quickly drew the bedraggled traveller inside; his saturated clothing was removed and before long John Bunyan was able to rest in a warm bed. But the damage was done. Not fully recovered from his earlier illness, he once again manifested symptoms of fever, as the chill and fatigue of his journey brought on a relapse. For several days his condition was far from good, but by Sunday, 19 August, the fever had abated. Bunyan rose thankfully from his bed, drained but feeling better. And only one thing was on his mind—his promise to preach in Whitechapel. He may have been unwise in his determination to carry on despite his health, but concern over disappointing the expectant people weighed heavily with him. Accompanied by Strudwick and others, Bunyan set out on the mile-long walk to his preaching appointment.

Usually reticent and thoughtful in company, Bunyan seemed unnaturally bright that day as they walked along. He had many things to say to his companions, and later they recalled some of his words and noted them down. Above all, they remembered the comments he had made on the trials of a Christian—and who better qualified to speak on such a subject than John Bunyan? 'Why do we find affliction so hard to bear?' someone had asked. 'Out of dark affliction comes a spiritual light,' John had replied, and added unforgettable words drawn directly from those hard early days of imprisonment:

> *In times of affliction we commonly meet with the sweetest experiences of the love of God. Did we heartily renounce the pleasures of this world, we should be very little troubled for our afflictions.*

The walk seemed short to Bunyan's friends, and soon they had reached the chapel. Relieved and thankful to see the well-loved preacher again, the congregation listened attentively as he addressed them on John 1:13. Although it was a short sermon, for the preacher was still far from well, it has been preserved because one of his hearers made extensive notes and later wrote up all he had heard. The burden of Bunyan's message was one that had concerned him through the years: the importance of holiness in the lives of those who professed faith. As he concluded he urged his hearers 'to live like the children of God, that you may look your Father in the face with comfort another day.'

And that 'other day' was close at hand for John Bunyan himself. On the Monday he probably had opportunity to see the first part of a new manuscript, *The Excellency of a Broken Heart*, through the press, but when he returned to the *Sign of the Star* he was struck down once more with fever. It would appear that Strudwick and other close friends who had gathered to spend time with him did not realize the serious nature of his condition because it does not seem that anyone thought of sending for Elizabeth or other members of his family.

At intervals John was still able to talk to those who gathered around his bed, and many of his sayings were carefully noted by those who came in and out of the room. But, as his condition deteriorated, his thoughts were gradually turning ever more often to the joys of a better world. He knew, even if his friends did not, that he had come to the brink of that bridgeless river which each must cross alone. Like Mr Valiant-for-Truth in Part 2 of *The Pilgrim's Progress*, John Bunyan had indeed been a fearless and noble pilgrim, constant to the end, and now he too could say:

> *My sword I give to him that shall succeed me in my pilgrimage, and my courage and skill to him that can get it. My marks and scars I carry with me, to be a witness for me that I have fought his battles, who will now be my rewarder.*

Those 'marks and scars' that John Bunyan would carry with him were created by unremitting government persecution, a weakened constitution after almost thirteen years spent in jail and the personal jibes and wicked innuendoes so often levelled against him by his enemies. These, together with his tireless endeavours in preaching and writing, had taken an exacting toll on his remaining strength. Not quite sixty years of age, he might well have expected to serve Christ's church for some years yet. Now he knew he must leave his family, his church and his friends behind. Would they be able to stand firm if persecution grew more intense once more? He did not know. Soon, however, all the trials of earth would be over for ever, not just for him but for them as well, and in anticipation of that day he exclaimed: 'O! what acclamations of joy will there be when all the children of God shall meet together without fear' (of persecution).

Despite the best attentions and concern that his friends could give, Bunyan's condition only worsened. Then all hope of recovery vanished. Now they could see he was dying. But Bunyan was well prepared for this day. Long years ago he had struggled against the fear of death; he had come to terms with the reality of it when he realised that his imprisonment might easily end in a verdict of public execution. In that crisis he had found that the only way to endure was to 'pass a sentence of death upon everything that can properly be called a thing of this life'. He had learnt 'to count the grave my home, to make my bed in darkness … that is to familiarise these things to me'. John Bunyan also knew, as the Shining Ones had told the trembling pilgrims before they entered the dark River, that the waters would prove 'deeper or shallower as you believe in the King of the place.'

During ten feverish days of illness John thought much about that city he had once glimpsed and those 'streets paved with gold.' Now he could declare with confidence to those who stood around, 'O! who is able to conceive the inexpressible, inconceivable joys that are there? None but they who have tasted of them!'

But those who watched by him could think of little else except the enormity of their loss. Tears streamed down their faces, for John Bunyan was dearly loved. Noticing their obvious distress, the dying man could only whisper, 'Weep not for me but for yourselves.' Then, as in the case of many other Christians brought face to face with death, that last and bitterest enemy, Bunyan's thoughts were clearly turning away from anything he might have been, had achieved, or even had suffered in his life. Only that solid foundation of his faith laid in the atoning sacrifice of Christ could give him confidence in the face of death:

> *I go to the Father of our Lord Jesus Christ, who will, no doubt through the mediation of his blessed Son, receive me, though a sinner; where I hope we ere long shall meet and sing the new song and remain everlastingly happy, world without end.*

These words, spoken with much difficulty but in assurance and hope, were his last. Far from his wife Elizabeth, far from his family and home, John Bunyan had crossed the last river. It was Friday, 31 August 1688. Once, as he had followed his pilgrims to the gates of the Celestial City, he had heard all the bells ringing out for joy and listened to the jubilant praises of those already there. Then he had 'wished myself among them'. Now God had granted his faithful servant his heart's desire.

A messenger was quickly dispatched to Bedford to carry the grievous news to Elizabeth and to the church. Meanwhile the funeral must go ahead, and on the following Monday, 3 September, the great preacher and writer was buried in a corner of Bunhill Fields graveyard known as 'Baptist Corner.' Situated off City Road in London, this graveyard was not attached to any parish church, and was one where thousands of plague victims had been hastily interred twenty-three years earlier. After the Act of Uniformity in 1662, a number of Nonconformists and Dissenters were also buried in Bunhill Fields. Certainly John Bunyan's grave, not far from that of his friend John Owen, was highly appropriate.

No details of Bunyan's funeral have survived—one which neither Elizabeth nor any family member could attended. John Strudwick, in whose home Bunyan had died, intended that when his own impressive family vault was next opened, John Bunyan's coffin should be removed from the corner where it was and placed within it—a suitable tribute to his friend. And this, it is generally supposed, took place ten years later when Strudwick himself died in 1698.

The imposing vault, standing not far from the entrance to Bunhill Fields, was restored in 1861. Complete with a new inscription to Bunyan and a life-sized figure of the preacher resting on it, it is a remarkable sight. In his hand is a book, and two emblems are carved on the sides of the grave: one of a man bowed beneath his burden; and the other of the same man as he loses his burden. This vault, shared with a number of members of John Strudwick's family, stands as a silent reminder to all who visit Bunhill Fields of the pilgrimage of life—one which John Bunyan trod both nobly and well—and always in hope of a glorious resurrection.